TWENTY FIRST CENT

SCI

GCSE Separate Sciences

Nuffield
Curriculum Centre

THE UNIVERSITY *of York*

OXFORD

The exercises in this Workbook cover the OCR requirements for each module. If you do them during the course, your completed Workbook will help you revise for exams.

Project Directors
Jenifer Burden
Peter Campbell
John Holman
Andrew Hunt
Robin Millar

Project Officers
Angela Hall
John Lazonby
Peter Nicolson

Course Editors
Jenifer Burden
Peter Campbell
Andrew Hunt
Robin Millar

Authors
Peter Campbell
Andrew Hunt
Caroline Shearer

Contents

B7 Biology across the ecosystem 4
C7 Chemistry for a sustainable world 38
P7 Observing the Universe 72

WORKBOOK B7, C7, P7

Great Clarendon Street, Oxford OX2 6DP

Oxford University Press is a department of the University of Oxford.
It furthers the University's objective of excellence in research, scholarship,
and education by publishing worldwide in

Oxford New York

Auckland Cape Town Dar es Salaam Hong Kong Karachi
Kuala Lumpur Madrid Melbourne Mexico City Nairobi
New Delhi Shanghai Taipei Toronto

With offices in

Argentina Austria Brazil Chile Czech Republic France Greece
Guatemala Hungary Italy Japan Poland Portugal Singapore
South Korea Switzerland Thailand Turkey Ukraine Vietnam

First published 2007

British Library Cataloguing in Publication Data

Data available

ISBN 978-0-19-915220-9

10 9 8 7 6 5 4 3 2 1

Printed in Great Britain by Bell and Bain Ltd, Glasgow

Illustrations by IFA Design, Plymouth, UK, and Q2A.

These resources have been developed to support teachers and students undertaking a new OCR suite of GCSE Science specifications, Twenty First Century Science.

Many people from schools, colleges, universities, industry, and the professions have contributed to the production of these resources. The feedback from over 75 Pilot Centres was invaluable. It led to significant changes to the course specifications, and to the supporting resources for teaching and learning.

The University of York Science Education Group (UYSEG) and Nuffield Curriculum Centre worked in partnership with an OCR team led by Mary Whitehouse, Elizabeth Herbert, and Emily Clare to create the specifications, which have their origins in the *Beyond 2000* report (Millar & Osborne, 1998) and subsequent Key Stage 4 development work undertaken by UYSEG and the Nuffield Curriculum Centre for QCA. Bryan Milner and Michael Reiss also contributed to this work, which is reported in: *21st Century Science GCSE Pilot Development: Final Report* (UYSEG, March 2002).

Sponsors
The development of Twenty First Century Science was made possible by generous support from:
- The Nuffield Foundation
- The Salters' Institute
- The Wellcome Trust

wellcometrust

THE SALTERS' INSTITUTE

Biology across the ecosystem B7

1 All organisms are dependent on energy from the Sun.

a Highlight or underline one word to describe the process of transferring energy from the Sun to chemical energy in organic compounds.

autotrophy	photosynthesis	synthesis	chlorophyll	enzyme

b In the diagram representing an ecosystem:

- colour **green** the box representing **autotrophs**
- colour **red** the box representing the **heterotrophs**
- add arrows to show the **transfer of energy** in this system

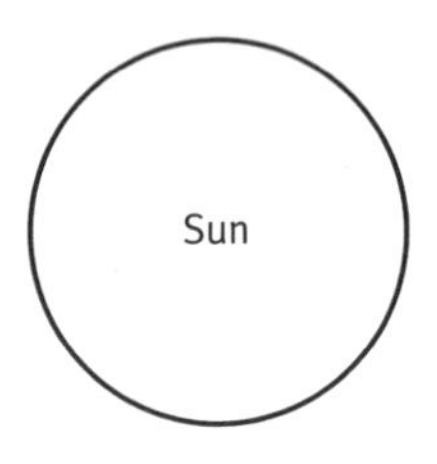

energy lost as heat

producers (plants)

consumer (feed off other living things)

c Give some examples of autotrophs and heterotrophs in these ecosystems.

Ecosystem	Examples of autotrophs	Examples of heterotrophs
broadleaved woodland		
motorway verge		
garden pond		
ocean		

d Explain how heterotrophs are dependent on energy from the Sun for their food.

....

....

e Some unusual bacteria can obtain energy from raw materials present in the environment. Highlight or underline the correct description of this type of bacteria.

autotrophy	heterotroph

2 Chloroplasts contain the green pigment chlorophyll and the enzymes that are needed for photosynthesis.

a Draw lines to match these key words with their meanings.

Key word	Meaning
carbohydrates	a carbohydrate, synthesized by plants using energy from light
chloroplasts	a carbohydrate, used by plants to store energy
chlorophyll	chemicals made of carbon, hydrogen, and oxygen
glucose	plant cell organelles where photosynthesis takes place
starch	the green pigment needed for photosynthesis

b Complete the word equation that sums up the process of photosynthesis.

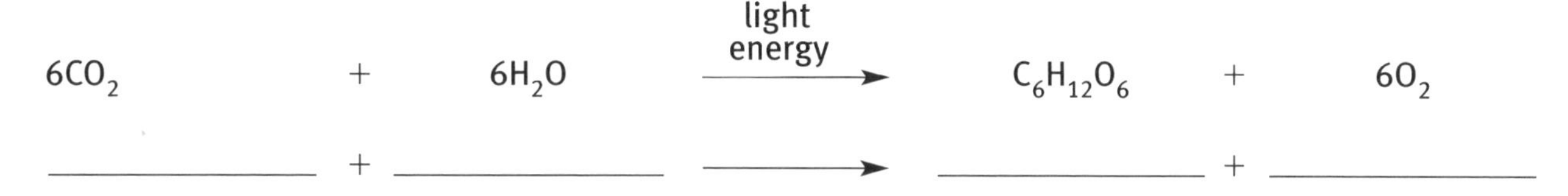

c Answer these questions about the main stages in photosynthesis.

i What chemical absorbs light energy?

....

ii How is the light energy used?

....

iii What sugar is produced?

....

iv What chemical is produced as waste?

....

d Only a small amount of the sunlight reaching a leaf is used for photosynthesis.
List two things that happen to the rest of the light energy reaching a leaf.

1 .... **2** ....

e Explain why nearly all plants look green.

....

....

3 Glucose made during photosynthesis is used by plant cells in three ways.

a Make notes for each heading to explain how plant cells use glucose. The words in the list should help.

cellulose	chlorophyll	energy	fat	protein	respiration	starch

glucose
$C_6H_{12}O_6$

growing:

storing energy:

releasing energy:

b A polymer has long molecules made up of chains of smaller units.
Write down the names of three polymers found in plant cells. (They can be found in the list above.)

1 .... **2** ....

3 ....

c Energy from cell respiration is used to synthesize polymers.

- Complete the diagram showing stages in the synthesis of plant cell polymers.
- Colour the arrows that use energy from respiration.

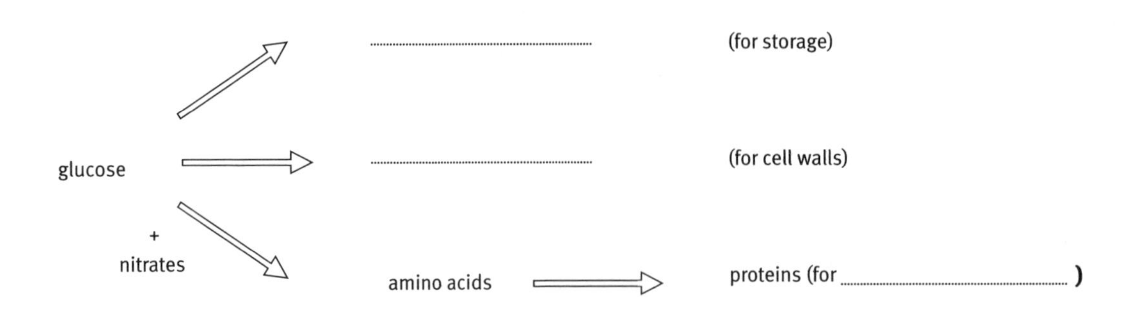

d Water can move across cell membranes by osmosis.
Add arrows to show how water would move between the cells shown.

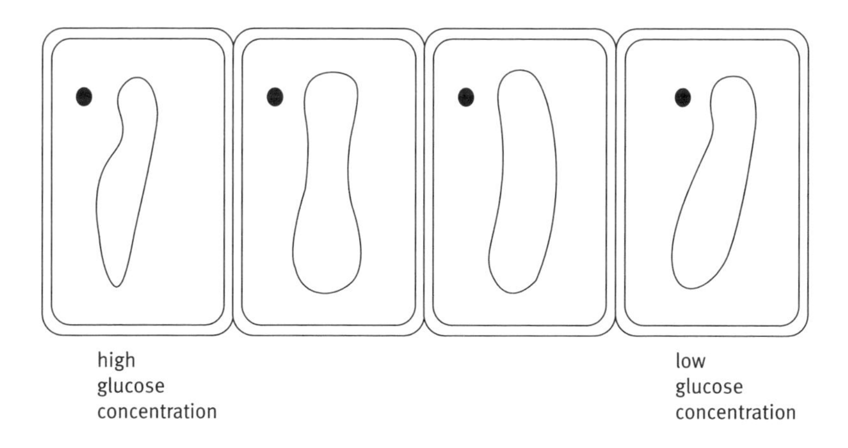

e Large carbohydrate molecules such as starch are insoluble. Explain why, for plant cells, starch is a better storage molecule than glucose.

....

....

f Use these words to complete the sentences.

active transport	diffusion	energy	protein

The nitrate ions needed for .... synthesis are taken in from the soil by plant roots.

To move nitrate ions into the cell, against the natural .... gradient, uses

.... This is an example of ....

g Complete the diagram to show the transport of nitrate ions into plant root cells.

- Add arrows to show the active transport of the nitrate ions.
- Add stars to show where energy is used in this process.

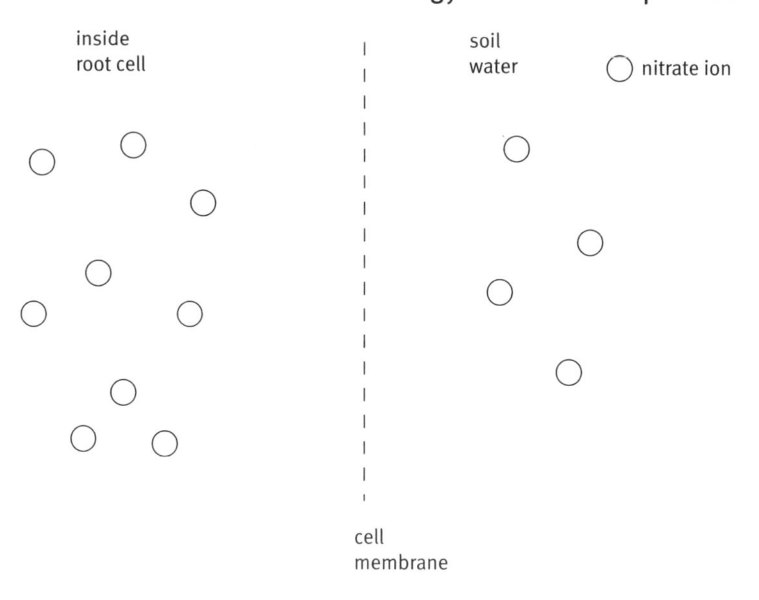

4 The rate of photosynthesis may be limited by several factors.

a Explain how the rate of photosynthesis will affect the growth of a plant.

....

b Look at the equation for photosynthesis (see question **2b**) and list four factors that could affect the rate of the process in a healthy plant.
(**Remember:** photosynthesis involves chemical reactions that are catalysed by enzymes.)

1 .... **2** ....

3 .... **4** ....

c Carbon dioxide forms 0.04% of air. The graph shows the effect of light intensity on the rate of photosynthesis in normal air at 20 °C. Use the graph to answer the questions.

i What is the main factor limiting photosynthesis at light intensity A?

....

ii What factors might be limiting photosynthesis at light intensity B?

....

iii Add and label a second line to the graph to show the effect of an increase in the carbon dioxide concentration to 0.1%.

iv Add and label a third line to the graph to show the effect of 0.1% carbon dioxide and an increase in temperature to 30 °C.

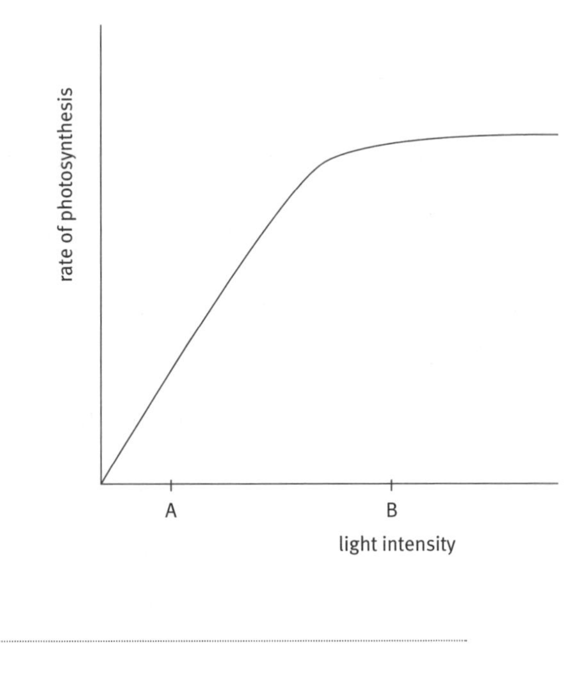

d A student collected data about the rate of photosynthesis in pondweed by counting the rate of bubble production under different conditions. Suggest some limitations of the student's data.

....

....

....

5 Some of the glucose produced during photosynthesis is used during respiration.

a Complete the word equation that sums up the process of respiration.

$C_6H_{12}O_6$ + $6O_2$ ⟶ $6CO_2$ + $6H_2O$ + energy

________ + ________ ⟶ ________ + ________ + ________

b The rates of photosynthesis and respiration in a plant were measured over 24 hours. Use the information in the graph to answer the questions.

i Describe how photosynthesis and respiration vary over 24 hours.

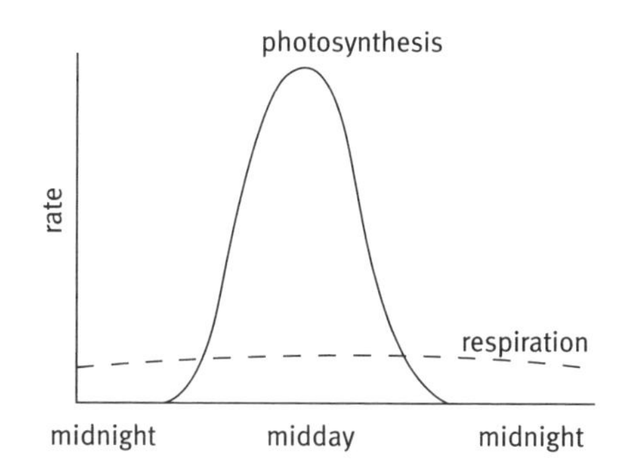

ii Fill in the table.

Chemical	Time of day showing net production	Time of day showing net use
oxygen		
carbon dioxide		
glucose		

iii The compensation point is when photosynthesis and respiration balance so that glucose is produced and used at the same rate. Label two compensation points on the graph.

iv What times of day do the compensation points occur?

c Most scientists agree that human activity is causing an increased level of atmospheric carbon dioxide. Fill in the table and then highlight or underline factors that are affected by human activity.

Factors that add CO_2 to the atmosphere	Factors that take CO_2 out of the atmosphere

6 Energy is transferred between organisms in an ecosystem.

a i Choose a type of ecosystem (such as field, woodland, pond, sea, or your own choice) and in the table with examples of organisms that would be found at different trophic levels in that ecosystem.

Ecosystem:	Trophic level	Examples of organisms
	producers	
	primary consumers	
	secondary consumers	
	tertiary consumers	
	decomposers	

ii Use some of these examples to construct a food chain.

producer → primary consumer → secondary consumer → tertiary consumer

.... → .... → .... → ....

iii Explain two ways that energy is transferred between organisms in this ecosystem.

1 ....

2 ....

b i The table shows data collected in a woodland ecosystem.

Woodland	Number of organisms	Biomass (mass units)
producers	5000	54 000
primary consumers	43 000	10 000
secondary consumers	4000	3000
tertiary consumers	1000	500

ii Sketch a pyramid of numbers for this woodland ecosystem.

iii Sketch a pyramid of biomass for this woodland ecosystem.

iv Explain what this data shows about feeding relationships in the food chain.

....

....

c Compare the two pyramids by filling in the table.

Comparisons	Pyramid of numbers	Pyramid of biomass
How easy is it to collect data?		
Does it give a good comparison of the trophic levels?		
What are the main advantages?		
What are some of the limitations		

d i The diagram represents the annual productivity of a sheep farming system. Add arrows to show the energy flow through the system.

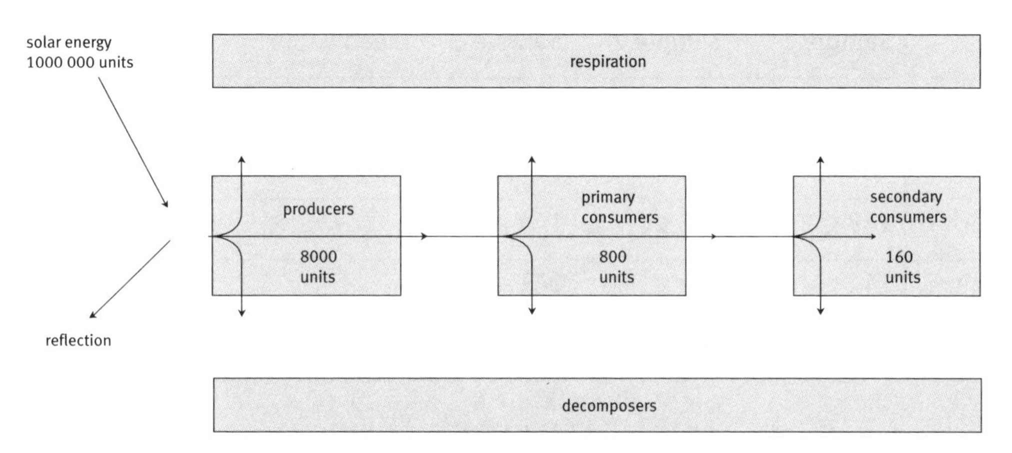

ii Where is the greatest loss of energy in the system?

....

iii If the producers in this system are grasses, the primary consumers sheep and the secondary consumers man, calculate:

- the percentage efficiency of energy transfer from solar energy to grass

$$\frac{\text{energy of grass}}{\text{solar energy}} \times 100 = \frac{\ldots\ldots}{\ldots\ldots} \times 100 = \ldots\ldots\%$$

- the percentage efficiency of energy transfer from grass to sheep ....

- the percentage efficiency of energy transfer from grass to man ....

iv This calculation has assumed that all the primary consumers are sheep. What other primary consumers might there be and how would they affect the energy efficiency calculations?

....

7 Soil is an important part of many ecosystems.

a Explain the importance, for plants, of the four main components of soil.

- inorganic particles (sand, silt, and clay) ....

- water (with dissolved mineral ions) ....

- air ....

- biomass (living and dead organisms) ....

b Use the data in the table (from several samples of the same soil) to answer the questions.

	Sample 1	**Sample 2**	**Sample 3**	**Mean value**
mass of fresh soil	200 g	200 g	200 g	
mass of dried soil	156 g	154 g	158 g	
mass after heating 5 min	148 g	152 g	144 g	
mass after heating 10 min	144 g	144 g	141 g	
mass after heating 15 min	144 g	146 g	139 g	

i Are there any outliers in the data that should be ignored or further investigated? Explain your answer. ....

....

ii Record the mean value for each measurement in the final column of the table. (Use these values for the following calculations.)

iii Calculate the percentage water in the soil sample.

$$\% \text{ water} = \frac{\text{mass of fresh soil} - \text{mass of dry soil}}{\text{mass of fresh soil}} \times 100 = \frac{\ldots\ldots}{\ldots\ldots} \times 100 = \ldots\ldots \%$$

iv Calculate the biomass as a percentage of the dry soil.

....

c Explain why the soil sample analysed in **b** could be described as a good fertile soil.

....

....

8 Heterotrophs have evolved a variety of feeding relationships.

a Complete the table and add several more examples.

Symbiotic relationship	The word that describes it	Examples
both organisms benefit	mutualism	sea anemone on the shell of a crab
	commensalism	moss on a tree
one organism gains at the expense of another organism		human tapeworm

b Describe the relationship between a host and a parasite.

c Explain why each of the features listed helps to make the tapeworm a successful intestinal parasite.

i A tapeworm has male and female sex organs.

ii A tapeworm produces a large number of eggs.

iii A tapeworm head has suckers and hooks.

iv A tapeworm has a large surface area.

v A tapeworm can use anaerobic respiration.

d Add notes to the diagram to explain the features that enable the malaria parasite to be successful.

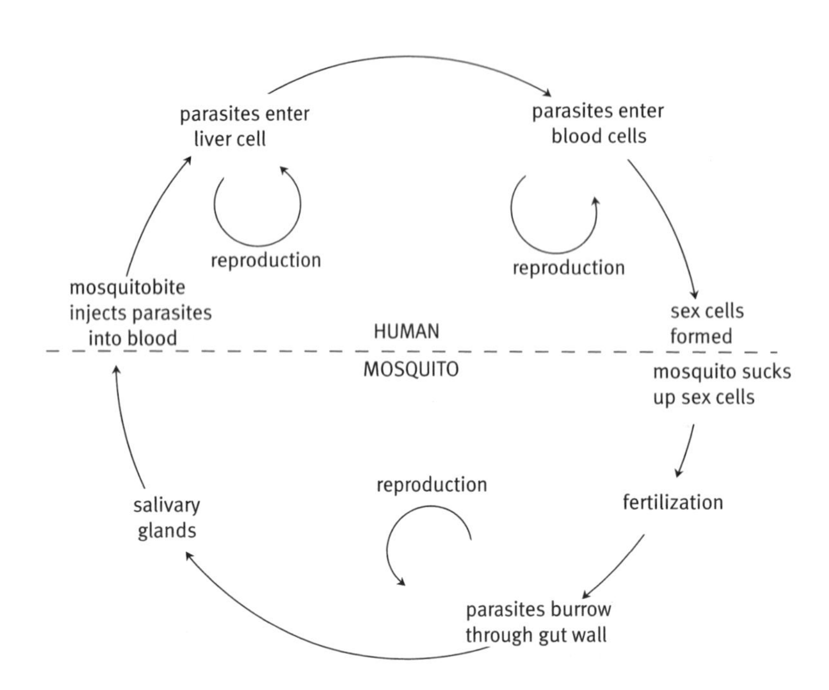

e Complete the table to describe some of the effects parasites can have on farm animals and crops.

Parasite	**Impact on food production**
roundworms in cattle and sheep	
potato blight (a fungus)	
fish lice on farmed salmon	
liver fluke in dairy cattle	
canker (a fungus) on apple trees	

f Explain why the evolution of a parasite is thought to be closely linked to that of its host.

9 Natural selection has resulted in an increased frequency of the sickle-cell allele in certain populations.

a Sickle-cell anaemia is caused by an allele of the gene which codes for haemoglobin. The sickle-cell allele is recessive. Use two colours and a key to show:

- members of this family who have sickle-cell anaemia
- members of this family who are carriers and have the sickle-cell trait (one normal allele and one sickle-cell allele)

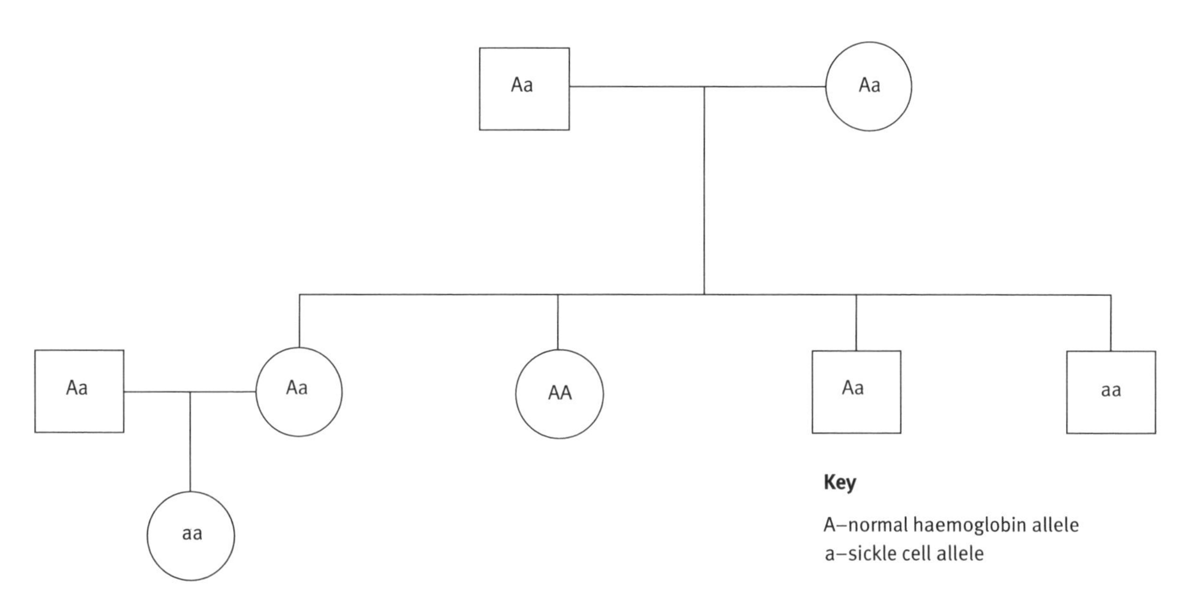

b What symptoms would someone who inherited two sickle-cell alleles show?

....

....

c Carriers of the sickle-cell allele have some protection from malaria.

i Explain how natural selection has led to the sickle-cell allele being rare in parts of the world where the malaria mosquito cannot survive.

....

....

....

ii Explain how natural selection has led to the sickle-cell allele being more common in parts of the world where malaria is a common cause of infant mortality.

....

....

....

10 Bacteria and fungi can be grown on a large scale to give useful products.

a Draw lines to match each key word with its meaning.

Key word	Meaning
antibiotic	a drug that stops the growth of, or kills, bacteria and fungi
enzyme	food protein obtained by growing microorganisms
fermentation	a group of single-celled fungi
single-cell protein	growing bacteria or fungi to make a useful product
yeasts	a protein that catalyses a chemical reaction

b Draw a bacterium and label the structures listed.

cell wall

cell membrane

circular DNA chromosome

DNA plasmid

c Give examples of products of traditional technologies:

- using yeast fermentation ....
- using an enzyme extract ....

d New technologies enable a wide range of products to be made by fermentation of carefully selected bacteria and fungi. Complete the table.

Type of product	**Examples**
antibiotics	
	Quorn, animal feed proteins
	rennin, amylase, pectinase, glucose isomerase

11 Genetically modified (GM) organisms are used to make new products or improve efficiency.

a In the diagram showing the genetic modification of a bacterium, add notes to describe the three main steps in the process.

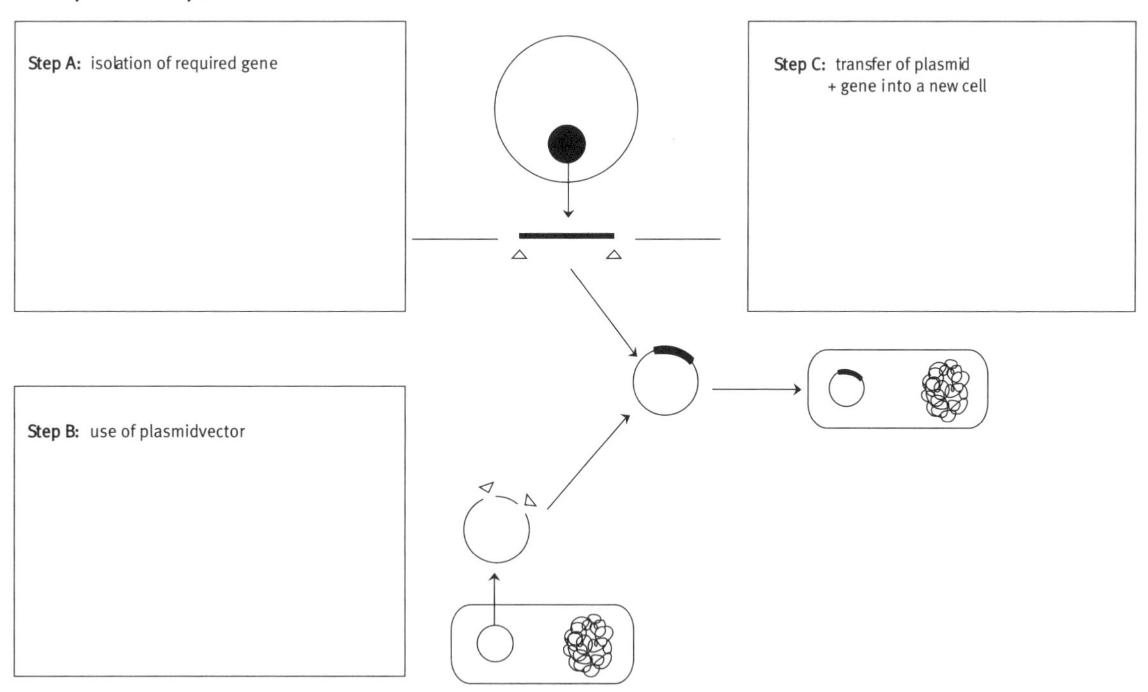

b Use these words to complete the sentences.

bacteriophage	plasmid	vectors

In the above example of genetic modification of a bacterium, the vector is a ....

A virus, such as a ...., is sometimes used as the vector during the genetic modification of bacteria. Viruses and bacteria are used as .... in the genetic modification of plants.

c Outline the main steps necessary to transfer gene X from a bacterium to sugar beet using a virus vector. The gene X makes the sugar beet more disease-resistant.

- **Step A** ....

  ....

- **Step B** ....

  ....

- **Step C** ....

  ....

d Use two different colours to highlight the types of organism used in fermentations (box 1).
Then use the colours to match them up with the useful products of fermentations (box 2).
(At least one product is made two alternative ways, so could be coloured with two different colours.)

1	2
GM fungi or bacteria	penicillin
natural fungi or bacteria	insulin
	alcohol
	Quorn
	rennin
	human growth hormone

---

12 There are economic, social, and ethical implications for the release of GM organisms.

a The potential risks of introducing GM organisms into the environment need to be balanced against the potential benefits. Use the table to summarize some of the arguments about the examples given.

	Arguments in favour	**Arguments against**
Question 1: Should a company be allowed to make a new antibiotic against tuberculosis in a fermentation system using GM bacteria?		
economic		
ethical		
social		
Question 2: Should farmers be allowed to grow insect-resistant maize from GM seeds?		
economic		
ethical		
social		

b Read about some of the implications of growing insect-resistant maize then answer the questions below.

A variety of maize has been genetically modified to be resistant to the European Corn Borer. This insect pest bores into maize plants causing them to fall over. In infested regions it can destroy 20% of the crop.

The pest is traditionally controlled using insecticide sprays. These work only during the first three days in the corn borer's life cycle, before it bores into the plant stem. The new variety of GM maize produces Bt toxin, which kills the corn borer. The Bt gene comes from a bacterium which is used as a biological insecticide by organic farmers.

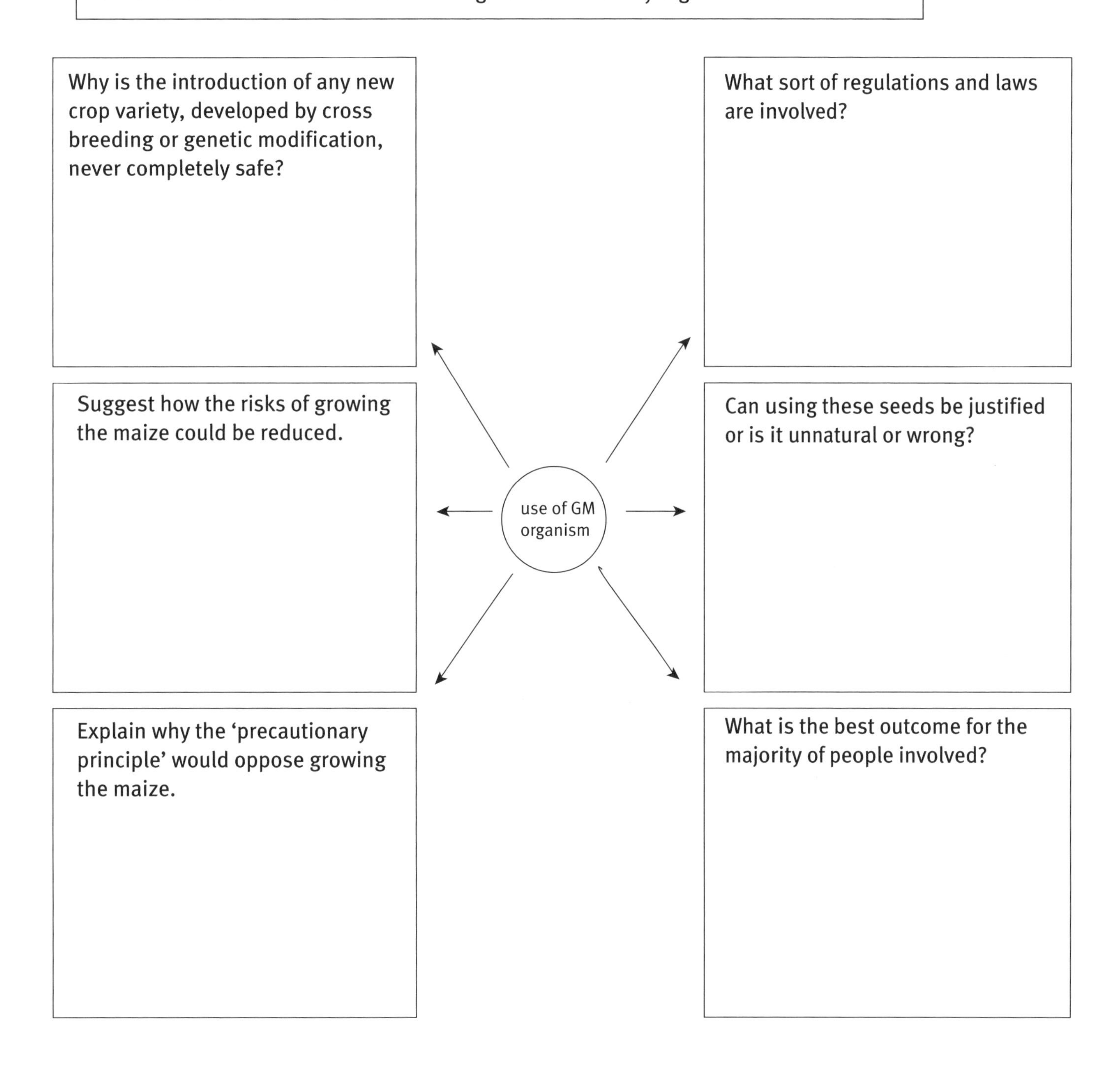

13 DNA can be extracted from cells for genetic tests.

a Genetic tests have been devised to provide information about a person's DNA. List some of the ways that information from genetic tests is used.

....

....

b DNA for a test is extracted from cells.

i Draw a simple diagram of a white blood cell, and label the features listed.

nucleus

cytoplasm

cell membrane

nuclear membrane

ii Where is the DNA in the cell? ....

iii What membranes must be opened to extract the DNA? ....

iv The DNA is then purified. What substances need to be removed from the cell extract?

....

v Why are red blood cells not used for DNA testing?

....

---

14 DNA technology is used to prepare gene probes for each test.

a A gene probe is a short piece of single-stranded DNA which has complementary bases to a DNA chain of the test allele. Add the correct bases to make a probe for the length of DNA shown.

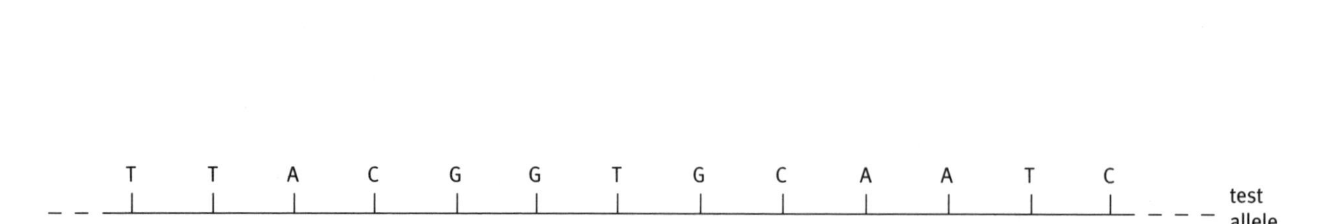

Remember: C pairs with G, T pairs with A

b Use these words to complete the description of how a gene probe works.

complementary	DNA	marker	stick

Genetic tests that use probes rely on the fact that when .... is gently heated and cooled the double strands separate and then rejoin. If this is done in the presence of a gene probe, the probe will .... to sequences of DNA in the test sample that are .... to the probe. The .... on the probe shows if this has happened.

c Markers for gene probes can be fluorescent or radioactive. Explain how the probes are detected in each case.

- Fluorescent probes: ....

  ....

- Radioactive probes: ....

  ....

d Explain the meaning of each of these terms used in DNA technology:

- gene ....
- allele ....
- gene probe ....
- autoradiography ....
- UV ....

15 Blood tissue has several different components.

a Match each blood component with the information about it using lines or colours.

Number of cells in 1 mm^3 of blood	Blood components	Function
7000	red blood cells	to transport water, solutes, and heat
250 000	white blood cells	to clot blood at injury sites
5 000 000	platelets	to fight infection
no cells (liquid)	plasma	to transport oxygen

b Draw the following cells, and label with notes to explain how they are adapted for their function:

a white blood cell

a red blood cell

c Draw lines to match these key words to their meanings.

Key word	Meaning
antibody	bloods that can be mixed without antigen–antibody problems
antigen	a marker on a cell surface that can cause antibody formation
blood transfusion	a person who receives blood from another person
compatible bloods	a protein that recognizes and binds to particular antigens
donor	the process of transferring blood from one person to another
recipient	a person who gives blood to another person

d Every person has one of four ABO blood types. The A, B, AB, or O blood types describe what ABO antigens are present on the red blood cells (A, B, both, or neither). There are also antibodies present in the blood plasma (anti-A and/or anti-B). Each blood type has antibodies against the ABO antigens that are not present on the red cells. Complete the table to show this.

Blood type	Antigens on the red cells	Antibodies in the plasma
A		
B		
AB	and	none
O	neither	and

e Blood is an important tissue and needs replacement after loss through accident or surgery. Blood transfusions are only possible between certain ABO blood types. The recipient must not have plasma antibodies against the red cell antigens in the donated blood.
Fill in the table:

- list the recipient antibodies present for each blood type
- add ticks ✓ or crosses ✗ to show if transfusion is possible for each donor/recipient combination

Recipient		Donor type A	Donor type B	Donor type AB	Donor type O
blood type	antibodies				
A					
B					
AB					
O					

f What blood type is the 'universal donor'? Explain what this means.

....

....

g What blood type is the 'universal recipient'? Explain what this means.

....

....

16 Your ABO blood type is determined by a single gene with three alleles.

a The three ABO alleles are I^A, I^B and I^O. The alleles I^A and I^B are codominant. The allele I^O is recessive to both. Complete the table to show how different pairs of alleles lead to the four ABO blood types.

Allele pair	Blood type
$I^A I^A$	
$I^A I^O$	
$I^B I^B$	B
	AB
	O

b Predict the possible blood types of children in the following families.

Family 1

	Father type A alleles $I^A I^O$	
Mother type A alleles $I^A I^O$	alleles blood type	alleles blood type
	alleles blood type	alleles blood type

Family 2

	Father type O alleles $I^O I^O$	
Mother type AB alleles $I^A I^B$	alleles blood type	alleles blood type
	alleles blood type	alleles blood type

c What chance is there of a child being blood type A in each of the above families?

- Family 1 ....
- Family 2 ....

d What ABO antibodies would be present in the blood plasma of the mother and father of family 2?

- Mother ....
- Father ....

17 The heart pumps blood around the body.

a Complete the table describing different parts of the heart.

Heart structure	**Description**
	receives blood from all parts of the body except the lungs
	pumps blood to the lungs
	receives blood from the lungs
	pumps blood to all parts of the body except the lungs
heart valves	

b In the above table:

- colour **red** the heart structures that are filled with **oxygenated** blood
- colour **blue** the heart structures that are filled with **deoxygenated** blood

c Complete these sentences.

Blood is carried towards the heart by blood vessels called ....

Blood is carried away from the heart by blood vessels called ....

d Valves are found in the heart and in veins.

- Draw a ring around the positions of the four heart valves.
- Explain what the valves in veins do.

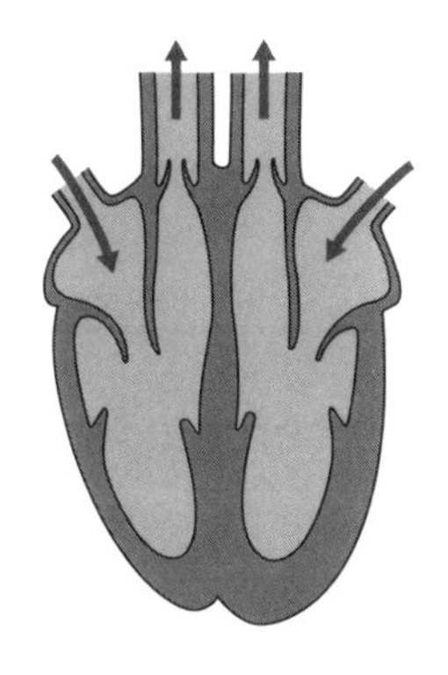

e Complete the diagram to show how the valves in veins work.

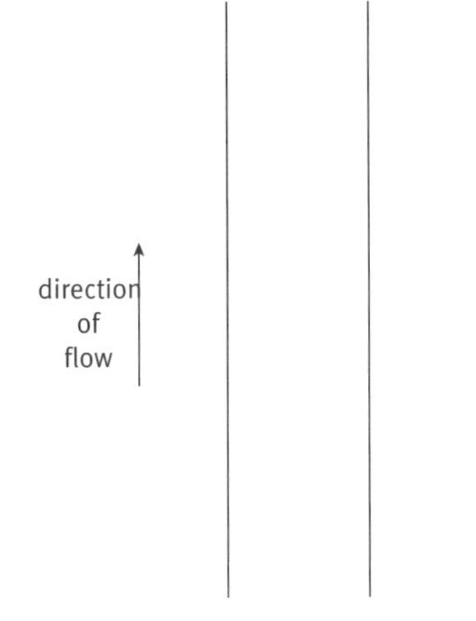

valve open allowing flow

valve closed preventing back flow

g In the flow chart:

- add arrows to show the double circulation of the blood around the body
- label the points where there is a capillary network

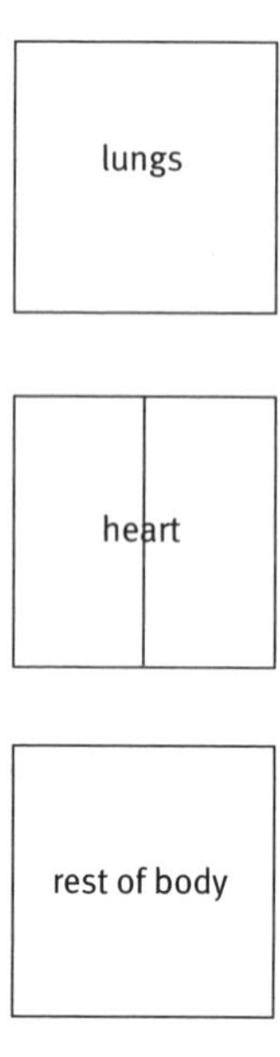

h Explain why a double circulation is important for oxygenated blood to reach all parts of the body.

....

....

---

18 Aerobic respiration provides most of the energy to your body cells.

a Write the word equation that summarizes the process of aerobic respiration, then answer the questions.

.... + ... → .... + ... + energy

i What is the body's source of glucose for respiration? ....

ii What is the body's source of oxygen for respiration? ....

iii How is the carbon dioxide waste removed from the body? ....

iv How is the glucose, oxygen, and carbon dioxide transported around the body? ....

....

b The exchange of chemicals between the blood and body cells takes place in the capillary beds and tissue fluids. Answer the questions about this process.

i How is the tissue fluid formed?

ii By what process are chemicals exchanged between the blood and body cells?

iii Name two chemicals passing from the blood into body cells.

iv Name a waste product from aerobic respiration passing from body cells into the blood.

v Name a waste product from protein and amino acid breakdown passing from liver cells into the blood (before being excreted by the kidneys).

c During exercise muscle cells need more energy. Explain how the following changes help to provide the extra energy needed by the muscle cells.

- The breathing rate increases.

- The heart rate increases.

d Explain why 'normal' measurements for heart rate and blood pressure cover a range of values.

19 Quick bursts of energy can be provided by anaerobic respiration.

a Anaerobic respiration can help to provide energy by using glucose but not oxygen. Write the word equation that summarizes anaerobic respiration.

.... → .... + energy

b Explain why anaerobic respiration can only be used by muscles for a short period of time.

....

....

c Oxygen is then needed to break down the lactic acid. Explain why this is called 'oxygen debt'.

....

....

d Summarize the differences between aerobic and anaerobic respiration by filling in the table.

	Aerobic respiration	**Anaerobic respiration**
What is the energy source?		
What else is needed?		
What waste products are formed?		
Compare the efficiency (which produces the most energy per molecule of glucose).		
Give some examples of when it is useful to the body.		
Describe the effects of increasing this respiration.		
Describe any after effects of increased respiration.		
Other notes		

20 For body movement, muscles need a supply of energy (as ATP) and a supporting framework.

a Use these words to complete the sentences.

ATP	currency	glucose	released	stored

All respiration releases energy from .... The energy is .... in the chemical ATP. Cell processes that require energy break down .... , energy is then .... ATP can be described as the energy .... of living things.

b A muscle is made up of hundreds of muscle fibres. Each muscle fibre is packed with protein filaments. Describe what happens to the fibres when a muscle is used to move a part of the body.

....

....

c Complete the flow chart to show the transfer of energy from glucose in the blood to the cells in a contracting muscle. Label the processes involved (include both aerobic and anaerobic respiration).

food energy as blood glucose

energy used in muscle contraction

d Draw lines to match these keys words to their meanings.

external skeleton	a living structure that provides a jointed framework to support movement, typical of vertebrates
internal skeleton	an animal with a backbone
vertebrate	a hard outer covering providing support and protection, may have flexible joints
invertebrate	an animal that does not have a backbone

e Give two examples of:

- invertebrates with an external skeleton

  1 .... **2** ....

- vertebrates with an internal skeleton

  1 .... **2** ....

f Describe some features of the human skeleton that help it to:

i provide support ....

....

ii protect the brain and spinal cord ....

....

iii allow movement ....

....

iv provide new blood cells ....

....

v store minerals ....

....

21 Movement of a joint depends on all its parts functioning effectively.

a i Draw two muscles that move the elbow joint on the diagram of the bones of the arm. Label the muscles A and B.

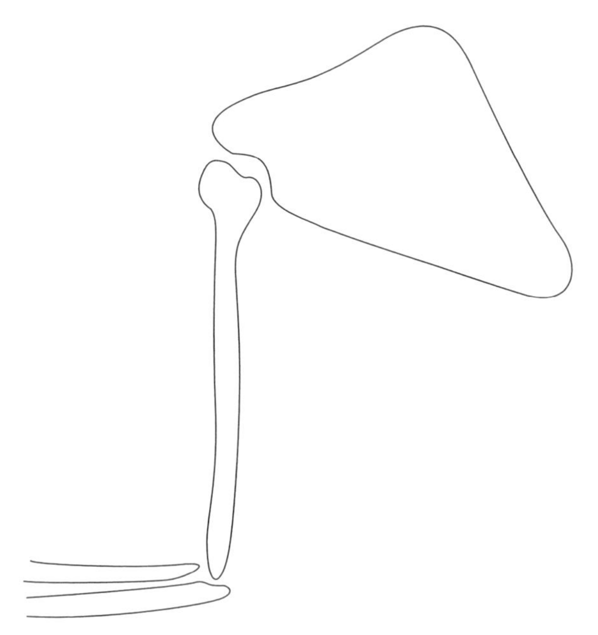

ii Explain what happens to each muscle when the lower arm is raised.

A .... **B** ....

iii Explain what happens to each muscle when the lower arm is lowered.

A .... **B** ....

iv These muscles are an antagonistic pair. Explain what this means.

....

....

v Describe an antagonistic pair of muscles from another part of the body.

....

b Draw lines to match these keys words to their meanings.

Key word	Meaning
cartilage	fluid lubricating and nourishing a joint
joint	tissue joining bones together
ligament	tissue joining muscle to bone
synovial fluid	smooth, shock-absorbing tissue protecting bones
tendon	where two or more bones meet

c Draw and label a joint between two bones showing: bones, ligaments, cartilage, synovial fluid.

d Explain the function of the synovial fluid.

....

e Specific properties of joint tissues enable them to function effectively. Complete the table:

- describe the function of each tissue
- use words from this list to describe some specific properties of each tissue

elastic (bouncy)		fibrous	flexible	not elastic
not stretchy	pearly	smooth	strong	white

Tissue	Function	Specific properties
cartilage		
ligaments		
tendons		

22 The correct treatment of skeletal-muscular injuries can help the healing process.

a Identify these common injuries from their descriptions.

dislocation	sprain	torn ligament	torn tendon

Description	**Injury**
tissue damage that results in an unstable joint	
tissue damage that results in loss of a certain movement	
an overstretched ligament	
displacement of a bone from its normal position in a joint	

b The most common sporting injury is a sprain. Complete the descriptions of the three main symptoms of a sprain.

1 Appearance (shape): ....

2 Appearance (colour): ....

3 ....

c The immediate treatment for sprains is RICE. Explain what each letter stands for, and describe what you would do to help someone who had sprained an ankle.

....

....

....

....

....

....

d Describe the sort of treatment that might follow a suitable period of RICE treatment.

....

....

e Describe the role of the physiotherapist in treatment of skeletal-muscle injuries. At what stage would a physiotherapist be involved? What sort of specialist help would a physiotherapist give to aid full recovery?

f Read the list of exercises recommended to someone recovering from a joint injury, then answer the questions below. Include references to muscles, tendons, and ligaments in your answers.

Exercise 1
Lie with your leg out straight. Tense up your thigh muscles, push your knee down, and try to raise your heel. Hold for a few seconds.

Exercise 2
Place a rolled up towel under your knee, keep your knee on the roll, and lift your heel. Try to get your knee completely straight.

Exercise 3
Bend your knee as far as it can easily go. Hold for a few seconds then straighten and repeat.

Exercise 4
Lie on your front. Keep your thigh down and bend your knee as far as you easily can.

i What do you think is the main purpose of these exercises?

ii Why do you think all the exercises are done lying down?

iii What would be the aim of exercises in the next stage of the recovery process? What sort of exercise might be recommended?

iv What would be the aim of exercises recommended for a final return to full fitness?

23 Physical training programmes can aid recovery from illness or injury, or improve fitness.

a Make a list of the sort of medical and lifestyle information that a trainer or medical professional would need to know about a client before recommending a training programme.

b Explain how a trainer working with an athlete would use their medical and lifestyle history.

c Explain how a hospital physiotherapist treating someone recovering from a joint operation would use their medical and lifestyle history.

24 Accurate record keeping during treatment or fitness training is essential.

a Health or fitness practitioners like to have regular contact with their patients or clients. Explain the advantages of this for:

- the health or fitness practitioner
- the patient or client

b Why does a fitness trainer need to know if their client starts a new course of medication?

c A good health or fitness practitioner team ensures 'continuity of care'.

i Explain the importance of accurate record keeping.

....

ii Explain the importance of the way those records are stored.

....

iii Explain the importance of allowing the right professionals access to the records.

....

d Describe an example of how the progress of a sportsman or sportswoman is monitored over a season of training. Give examples of what measurements would be taken and recorded.

....

....

....

....

---

25 Good training programmes include assessment, modification, and follow up.

a Treatments often have side effects which have to be weighed up against the benefits. Add examples of possible benefits and side effects for the treatments suggested in the table.

Suggested treatment	Possible benefits	Possible side effects
A a gym workout programme for an overweight person (Target: weight in the 'normal' range)		
B a walking programme for a patient with heart problems (Target: improved cardiovascular fitness)		
C a very strict, intensive training schedule for an athlete (Target: optimum fitness for a particular event)		

b Choose two of the examples (A, B or C) in the table, and for each suggest why the programme might need to be modified before it has been completed.

- Example .... : ....

....

- Example .... : ....

....

c Choose two of the examples in the table, and for each suggest another way of achieving the target.

- Example .... : ....

....

- Example .... : ....

....

d If the patients/clients in the table achieved their targets, suggest how their progress could then be monitored.

A ....

B ....

C ....

e Assessment of progress needs to take into account the reliability of the data obtained. Explain what problems there might be with data obtained in these situations.

- **Example A** (in the table) occasionally measuring his/her weight at home using bathroom scales.

....

- **Example B** having blood pressure and pulse measured weekly by a visiting nurse who calls at a different time each week.

....

- **Example C** doing regular timed runs on an outside track in different weather conditions.

....

1 Methane molecules

Complete this table, which shows three ways of picturing a molecule of methane. Add these terms in the correct places as column headings:

- ball-and-stick model
- molecular formula
- structural formula

CH_4		[ball-and-stick model of methane]

2 Alkane formulae

Complete this table by adding the missing information about three alkanes.

Name	Molecular formula	Structural formula
	C_2H_6	
		H–C(H)(H)–C(H)(H)–C(H)(H)–H
butane		

3 Burning alkanes

Many fuels contain alkanes. Alkanes burn in air. They react with oxygen. Write a balanced equation, with state symbols, for the reaction of ethane burning in plenty of air.

....

4 Alkane properties

Use the terms in the box to complete the summary of the properties of alkanes.

alkane	crude oil	gases	hydrocarbons	oily	single bonds	water

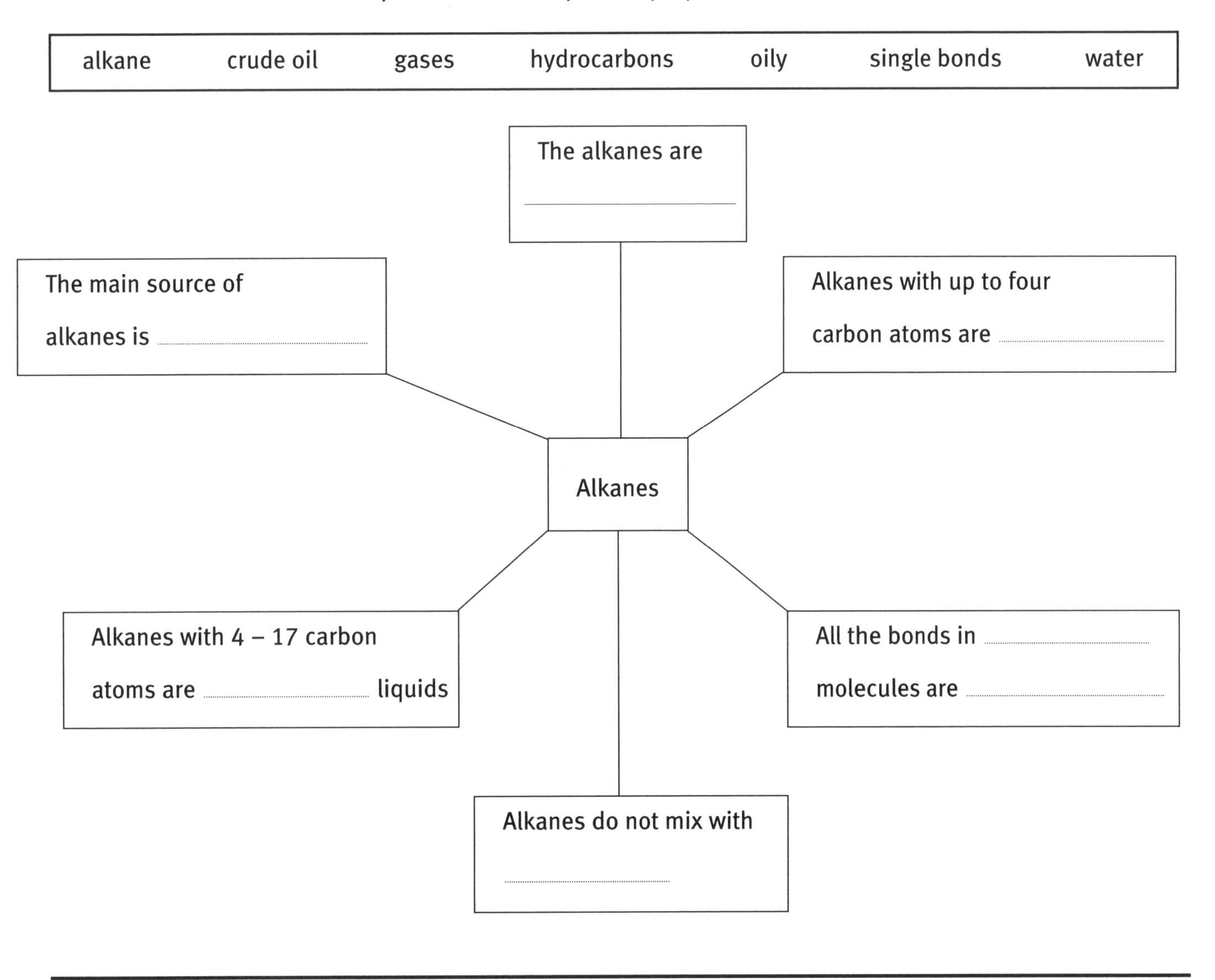

5 Alkane structure and reactivity

Add notes and labels to this diagram to explain why alkanes do not react with common laboratory reagents, such as acids and alkalis.

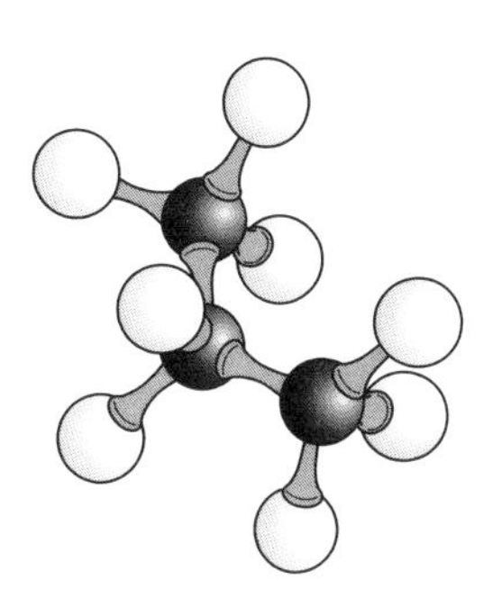

6 Methanol and ethanol

Complete this table. In the models, colour the carbon atoms black and the oxygen atoms red.

	Methanol	**Ethanol**
Molecular formula		
Ball-and-stick model		
Examples of uses		

7 Alcohols compared to water and alkanes

Complete this table to compare methanol with water and methane. In the models, colour the carbon atoms black and the oxygen atoms red.

	Water	**Methanol**	**Methane**
Molecular formula			
Ball-and-stick model			
State at room temperature			
Boiling point			−161 °C
Ease of mixing or dissolving in water			
Explanation in terms of the strength of the attraction between molecules			

8 Functional groups

In this diagram of an ethanol molecule, colour the carbon atoms black and the oxygen atoms red. Label and annotate the diagram to show:

- the functional group
- the bonds which are reactive
- the bonds which are not reactive.

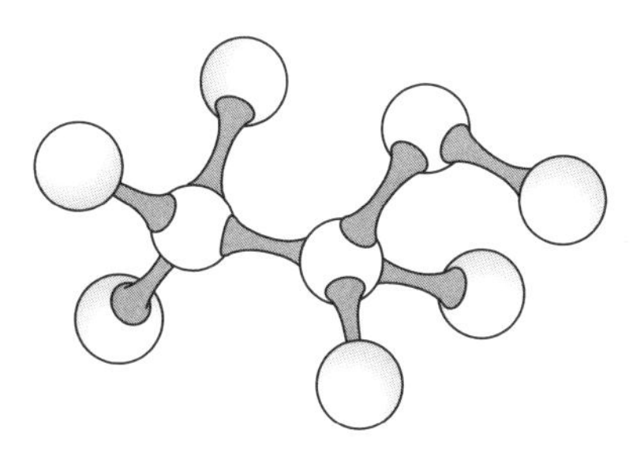

9 Reactions of alcohols

a In some ways alcohols are like water. However, alcohols burn and water does not. Explain why alcohols can burn and state the products of burning if there is plenty of air.

....

....

....

....

b Write a balanced equation for the reaction of ethanol burning in air.

....

c Complete this table to compare the reactions of three chemicals with sodium.

	Water	**Methanol**	**Methane**
Does the chemical react with sodium? If yes, what are the products?			
Formula of the product that contains sodium (if there is one)			

10 Natural occurrence of organic acids

Draw lines to link the names of carboxylic acids to where they can be found naturally.

Acid		Where found
Acetic acid (ethanoic acid)		In the fats of goats milk and in stale sweat
Butyric acid (butanoic acid)		Orange and lemon juice
Caproic acid		Rancid butter and vomit
Citric acid		Sour milk
Lactic acid		Vinegar

11 Reactions of carboxylic acids

Complete these word equations to show the typical reactions of organic acids with metals, metal oxides, and hydroxides, and metal carbonates.

methanoic acid + ... → magnesium methanoate + hydrogen

methanoic acid + sodium hydroxide → .... + ...

ethanoic acid + ... → copper ethanoate + water

ethanoic acid + potassium carbonate → .... + ... + ...

12 pH of solutions of acids

Draw lines to match each solution to its pH value. Some solutions listed have the same pH value.

Solution		pH value
Dilute acetic acid (ethanoic acid)		pH 7
Dilute hydrochloric acid		pH 3
Vinegar		pH 1
Pure water		

13 Carboxylic acid formulae and structures

a Complete this table. In the models, colour the carbon atoms black and the oxygen atoms red.

	Methanoic acid	**Ethanoic acid**
Molecular formula		
Structural formula		
Ball-and-stick model		

b What is the functional group in an organic acid?

....

....

c i Write a symbol equation to show how ethanoic acid ionizes when it dissolves in water.

ii Which of the products of the ionization of ethanoic acid makes the solution acidic?

d Draw a ring round the formulae below that represent carboxylic acids.

CH_3OCH_3 $HCOOH$ $CH_3CH_2CH_2CH_2OH$ $CH_3CH_2CH_2COOH$

14 Esters

a Give one word to describe the typical smell of many simple esters.

....

b Give examples of **three** foods we eat that taste of mixtures of esters.

....

c Give two uses of esters.

- ....
- ....

d Use the names of the chemicals in the box below to write a word equation for the formation of an ester.

water	ethanol	ethyl butanoate	butanoic acid

....

e Complete this word equation:

pentanol + ethanoic acid → .... + ...

f Label the diagrams below to show how to make a small sample of an ester and then smell the product.

The words in the box will help you.

acid	alcohol	catalyst	carboxylic acid	hot water
neutralize leftover acid	reaction of mixture after warming	sodium carbonate solution		

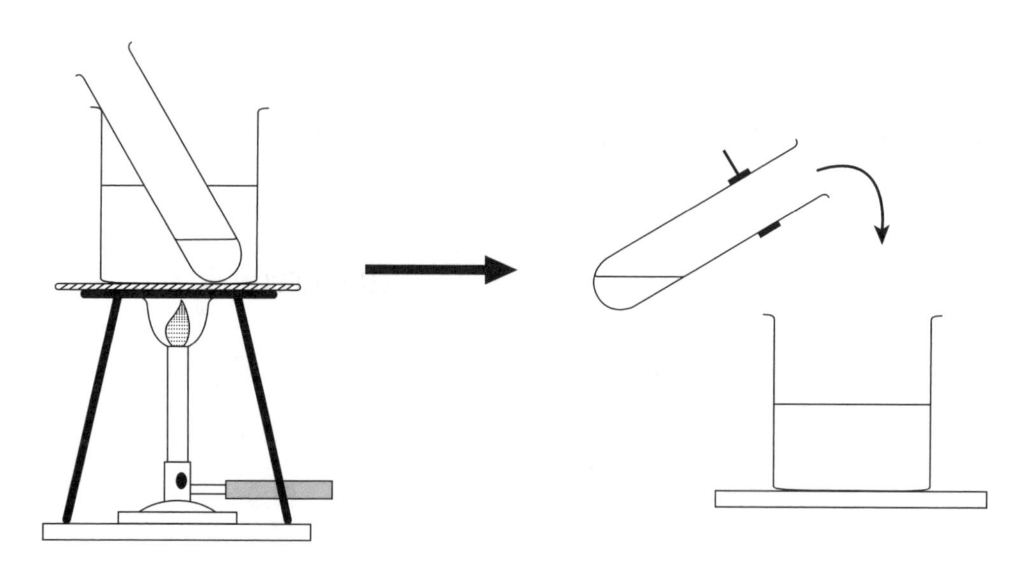

15 Preparation of an ester

This flow diagram shows the procedure used to make a sample of an ester on a laboratory scale.

Annotate (label) the diagram. The words in the box below will help you. You may choose to use some words more than once.

aqueous reagent to remove impurities	catalyst	drying agent	ethanoic acid
ethanol	ester from tap funnel	heat	impure ester layer
concentrated sulfuric acid	distillation flask	impure product	pure ethyl ethanoate
reflux condenser	tap funnel	thermometer	water condenser

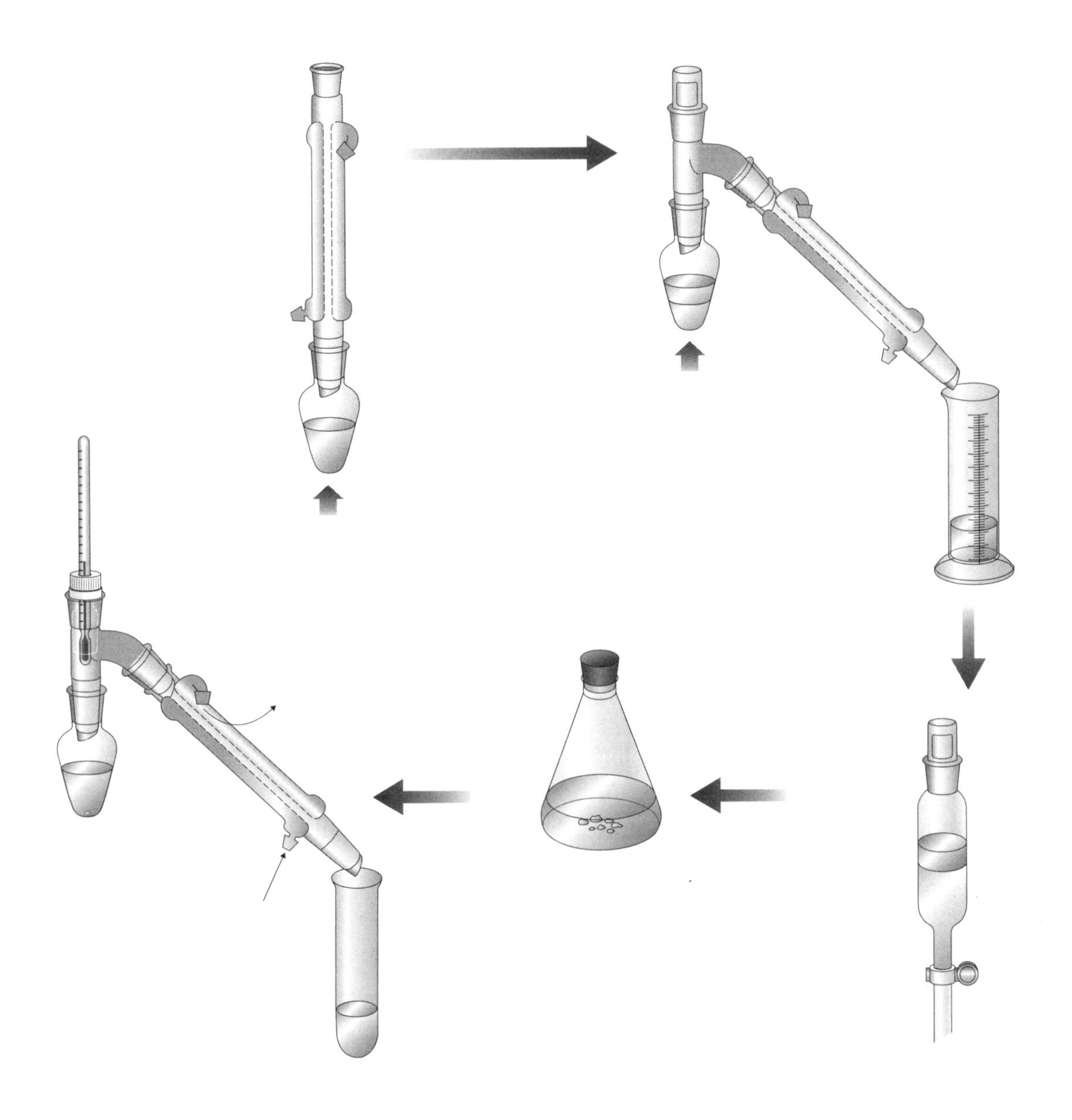

16 Fats and oils

a Why are fats and oils important to plants and animals?

....

b These diagrams show the structures of a molecule from a fat and a molecule from an oil. Label both diagrams to show: an ester link, a hydrocarbon chain, and the part of the molecule which comes from glycerol.

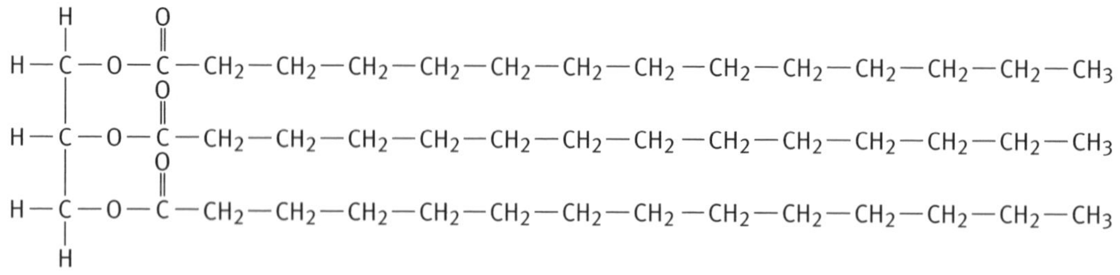

```
    H      O
    |      ||
H — C — O — C — CH2—CH2—CH2—CH2—CH2—CH2—CH2—CH2—CH2—CH2—CH2—CH2—CH3
    |      O
    |      ||
H — C — O — C — CH2—CH2—CH2—CH2—CH2—CH2—CH2—CH2—CH2—CH2—CH2—CH2—CH3
    |      O
    |      ||
H — C — O — C — CH2—CH2—CH2—CH2—CH2—CH2—CH2—CH2—CH2—CH2—CH2—CH2—CH3
    |
    H
```

Diagram A

```
    H      O
    |      ||
H — C — O — C — CH2—CH2—CH2—CH2—CH2—CH2—CH2—CH=CH—CH2—CH=CH—CH2—CH=CH—CH2—CH3
    |      O
    |      ||
H — C — O — C — CH2—CH2—CH2—CH2—CH2—CH2—CH2—CH=CH—CH2—CH=CH—CH2—CH=CH—CH2—CH3
    |      O
    |      ||
H — C — O — C — CH2—CH2—CH2—CH2—CH2—CH2—CH2—CH=CH—CH2—CH=CH—CH2—CH=CH—CH2—CH3
    |
    H
```

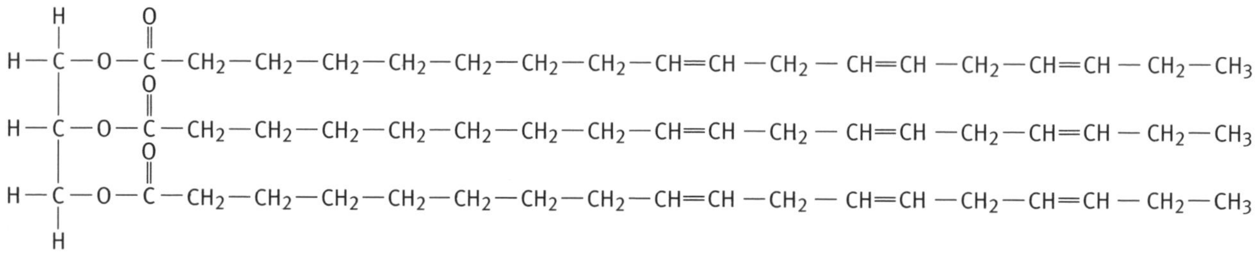

Diagram B

c Are the hydrocarbon chains in molecule A saturated or unsaturated? Is this the structure of a molecule from a fat or an oil? Give your reasons. ....

....

....

....

....

d Are the hydrocarbon chains in molecule B saturated or unsaturated? Is this the structure of a molecule from a fat or an oil? Give your reasons. ....

....

....

....

....

17 Exothermic reactions

a The reaction of magnesium with dilute hydrochloric acid is an exothermic reaction. Use the words in the box to label the diagram below, and explain what is meant by the term 'exothermic reaction'.

dilute hydrochloric acid	energy given out	exothermic	magnesium
magnesium chloride solution			

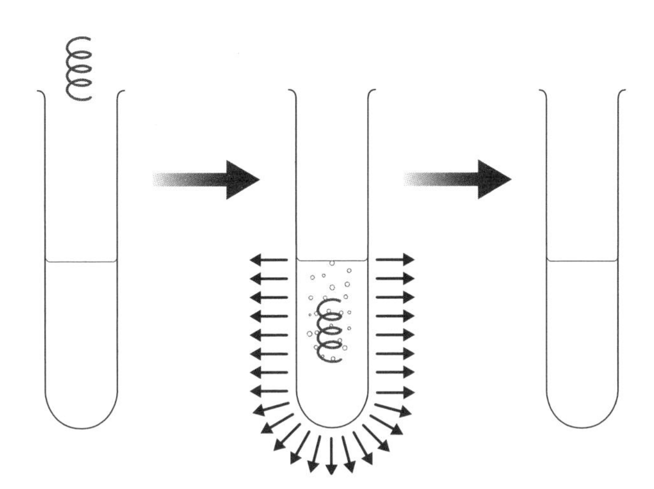

b Write a balanced symbol equation, with state symbols, for the reaction of magnesium with dilute hydrochloric acid.

....

c Use parts of the symbol equation to label the energy level diagram below by adding the reactants and products to the diagram. Complete the labelling of the diagram.

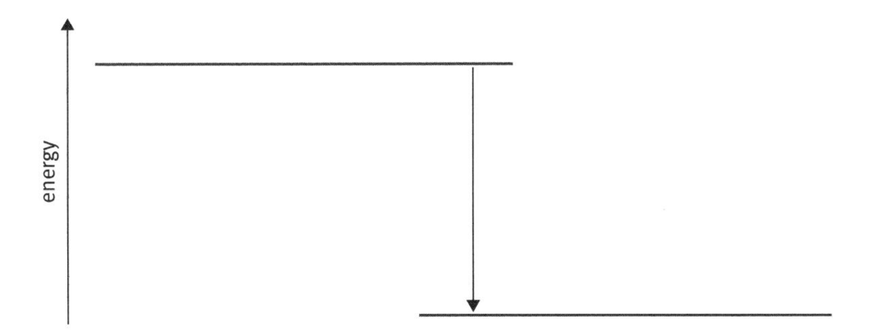

d Give two more examples of exothermic changes:

- ....
- ....

18 Endothermic reactions

a The reaction of citric acid with sodium hydrogencarbonate is an endothermic reaction. Use the words in the box to label the diagram below, and explain what is meant by the term 'endothermic reaction'.

citric acid	endothermic	energy taken in	sodium citrate solution
sodium hydrogencarbonate			

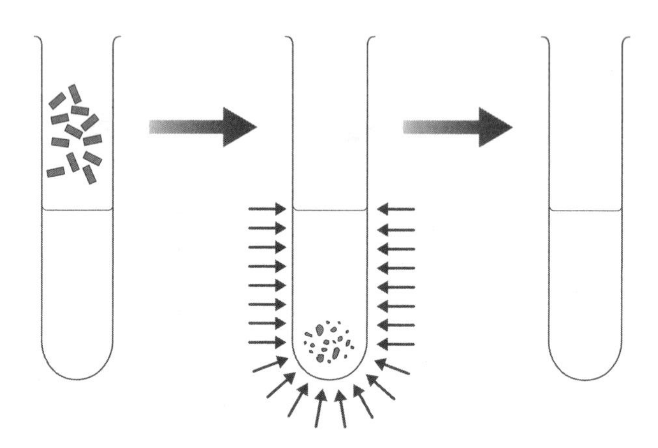

b Write a word equation, with state symbols, for the reaction of citric acid with sodium hydrogencarbonate.

....

c Use parts of the word equation to label the energy level diagram below by adding the reactants and products to the diagram. Complete the labelling of the diagram.

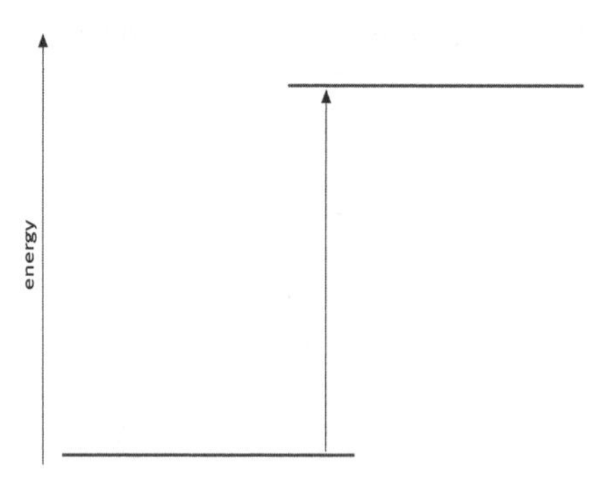

d Give two more examples of endothermic changes:

- ....
- ....

19 Bond breaking and bond forming

a Use the words in the box to label the diagram below. Colour the oxygen atoms red.

bond broken during reaction	bond formed during reaction	hydrogen molecule
oxygen molecule	water molecule	

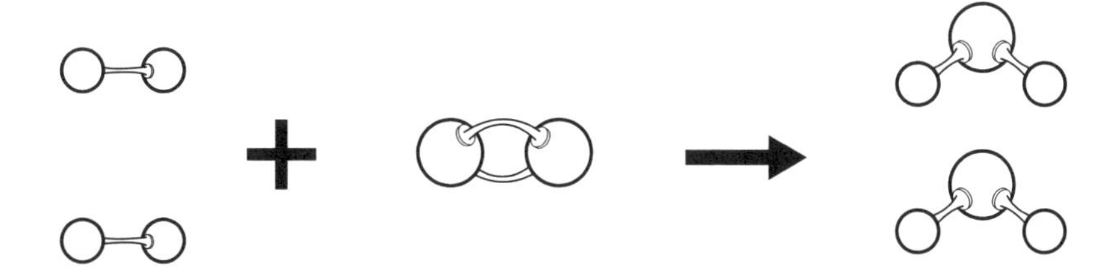

b Explain why the reaction of hydrogen with oxygen is an exothermic reaction.

....

....

c Use the data in the table to complete the labelling of the diagram below.

Process	Energy change for breaking all the bonds in the formula mass of the chemical
Breaking all the H—H bonds in hydrogen	434 kJ needed
Breaking all the Br—Br bonds in bromine	193 kJ needed
Breaking all the H—Br bonds in hydrogen bromide	366 kJ needed

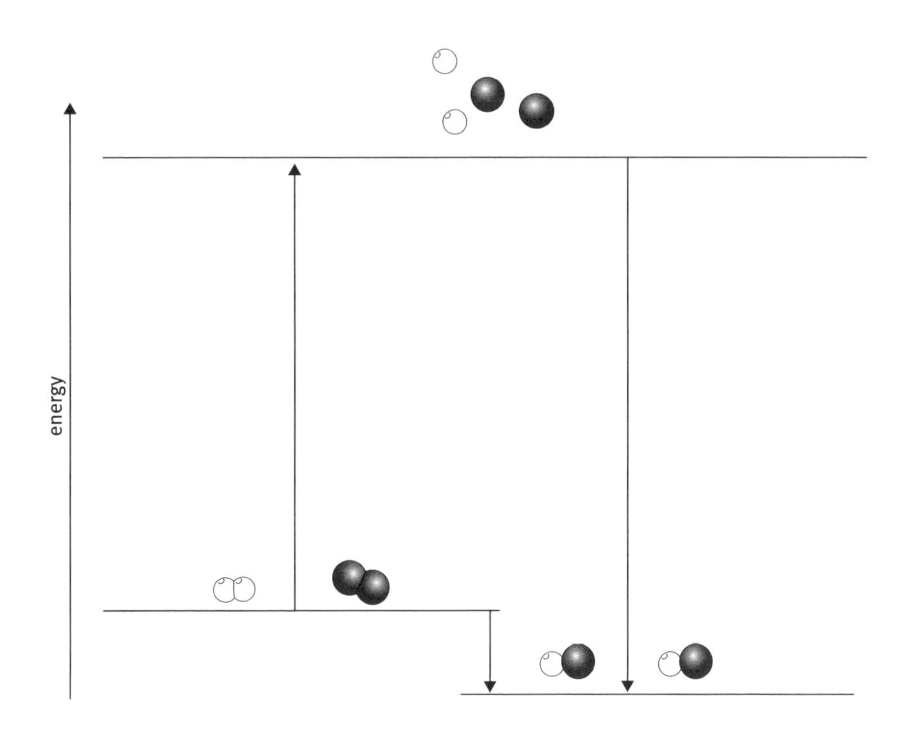

20 Activation energies

a With the help of some or all of the words and phrases in the table, write a paragraph to explain what is meant by the term activation energy.

new bonds form	high energy	bonds break	unsuccessful collision
reactant molecules	millions of collisions per second	low energy	collisions
not all collisions lead to reaction	minimum energy	successful collision	product molecules

....

....

....

....

....

....

....

....

....

....

b Use the idea of activation energy to explain why reactions go faster as the temperature rises.

....

....

....

....

....

....

21 Reversible changes

a For each of these pairs of equations, indicate the conditions needed to make the change go in the direction shown in the equation.

Conditions needed to make the change happen in the direction shown:

$H_2O(l) \rightarrow H_2O(g)$ ....

$H_2O(g) \rightarrow H_2O(l)$ ....

$CuSO_4.5H_2O(s) \rightarrow CuSO_4(s) + 5H_2O(l)$ ....

$CuSO_4(s) + 5H_2O(l) \rightarrow CuSO_4.5H_2O(s)$ ....

$NH_3(g) + HCl(g) \rightarrow NH_4Cl(s)$ ....

$NH_4Cl(s) \rightarrow NH_3(g) + HCl(g)$ ....

b Hot iron reacts with steam to form the iron oxide, Fe_3O_4 and hydrogen.

Write a balanced symbol equation for the reaction.

....

This reaction is reversible. Label the diagram to show how to demonstrate the reverse reaction.

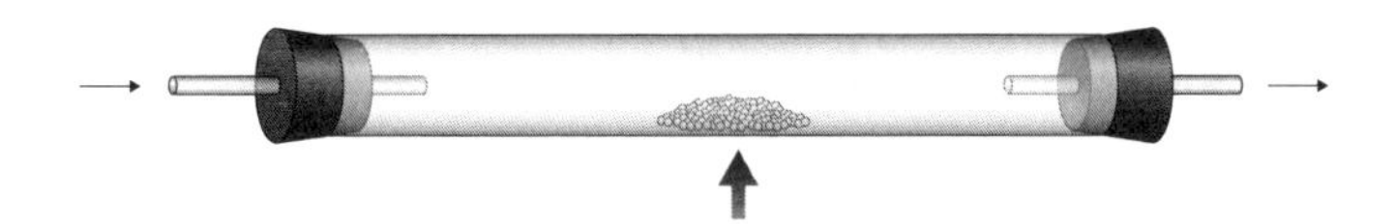

Write a balanced symbol equation for the reverse reaction.

....

22 Dynamic equilibrium

a The diagram below shows a crystal of iodine dissolving in hexane. The solution formed is then shaken with a solution of potassium iodide in water. Colour the solutions.

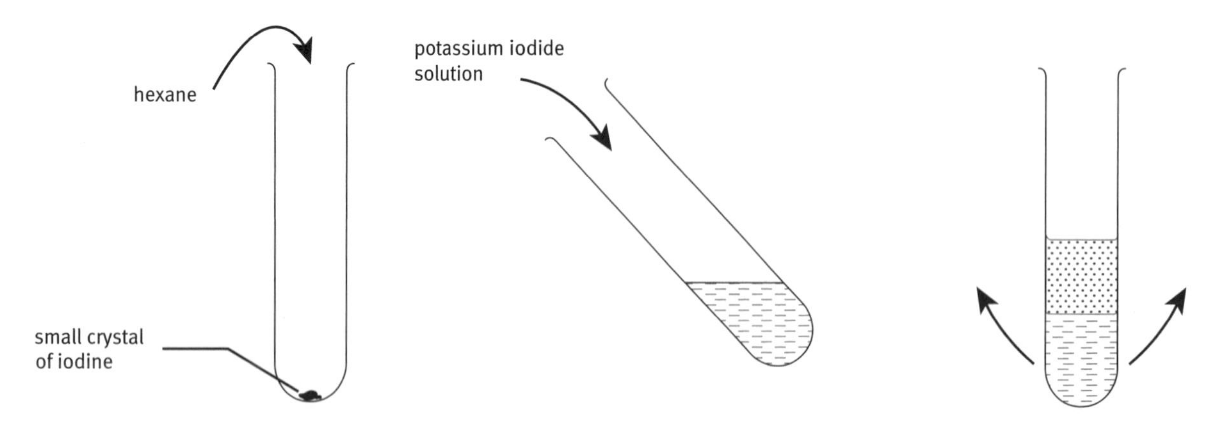

Explain why there is some iodine in both layers, however long the two solutions are shaken up together. ....

....

....

b The diagram below shows a crystal of iodine dissolving in aqueous potassium iodide. The solution formed is then shaken with hexane. Colour the solutions.

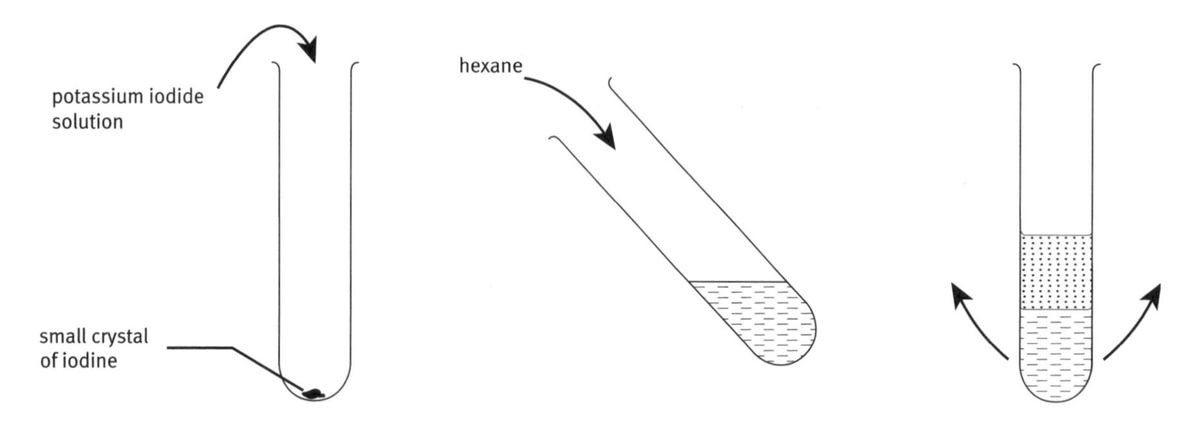

Explain why the two layers look the same after shaking as they did when the crystal was first dissolved in hexane and then shaken with potassium iodide solution. ....

....

....

c Why is the term 'dynamic equilibrium' used to describe the state reached when solutions of iodine in hexane and in aqueous potassium iodide are shaken up together? ....

....

....

23 Dynamic equilibrium on a molecular scale

The diagrams below show what happens to iodine molecules on shaking a solution of iodine in hexane (violet) with a solution of potassium iodide in water (which starts colourless). Colour the diagrams. Under each diagram explain what is happening to the molecules.

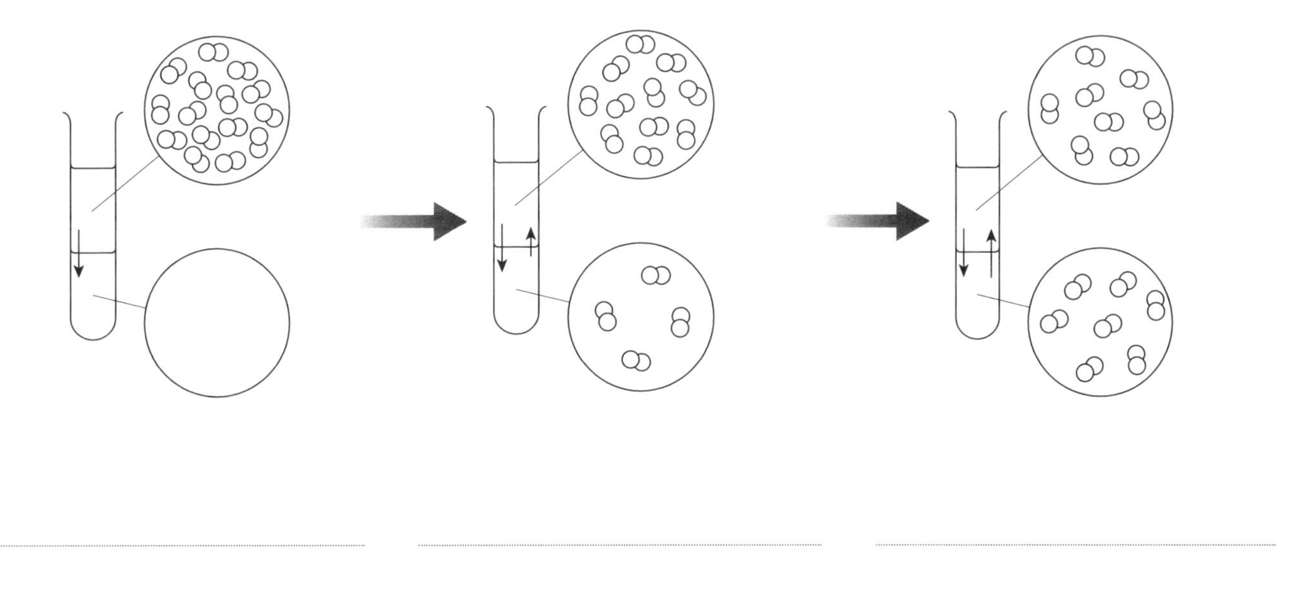

24 Strong and weak acids

Fill in the blanks to complete these sentences and equations.

- Hydrogen chloride gas dissolves in water to give a solution of ________ acid.

  $HCl(g)$ + water → ________ (aq) + $Cl^{-}(aq)$

- All of the molecules of hydrogen chloride ionize when the gas dissolves in ________.

  Hydrogen chloride is a ________ acid. Another example of a strong acid is

  ________ acid.

- Carboxylic acids are ________ acids. In a dilute solution of ethanoic acid, only about one molecule in a hundred ionizes. In solution there is a dynamic ________.

  $CH_3COOH(aq) + H_2O(l) \rightleftharpoons CH_3COO^{-}(aq) +$ ________ (aq)

25 Sampling for analysis

a When taking samples for analysis, it is important to make sure that they are typical of the whole bulk of the material analysed. Analysts have to decide:

- how many samples to collect, and how much of each to collect, to be sure that the samples are representative
- how many times to repeat an analysis on a sample to be sure that the results are reliable
- where, when and how to collect samples of the material
- how to store samples and take them to the laboratory to prevent samples 'going off', becoming contaminated, or being tampered with.

Write down the main issues for the person planning the analysis of the following materials.

i Soil in a farmer's field

ii Water in a pond

iii Polluted air in a city street

iv Urine from an athlete

b Give reasons why it is important to have standard procedures for collecting, storing and analysing samples.

26 Paper and thin-layer chromatography

a Label this diagram. It may help to use colours.

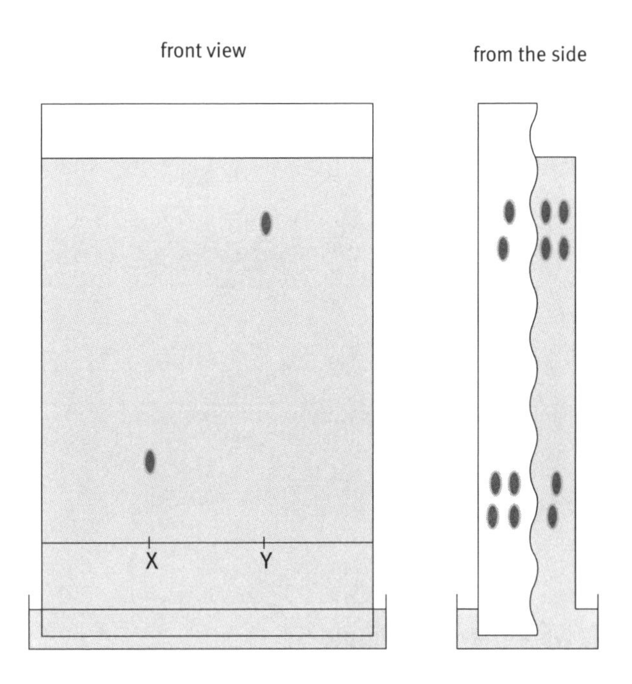

- Label the mobile phase, stationary phase and solvent front.
- Add an arrow to show the direction in which the solvent front moves.
- Add arrows to show that for both chemicals in samples X and Y there is a dynamic equilibrium between the stationary phase and the mobile phase.

i What would happen to a spot of substance on the start line that is not at all soluble in the mobile phase?

....

ii Explain why sample Y moves further than sample X.

....

....

b Complete this table to compare paper and thin-layer chromatography

	Paper chromatography	**Thin-layer chromatography**
Stationary phase		
Mobile phase		
Speed of separation		
Quality of separation		
Qualitative or quantitative?		

27 Interpreting chromatograms

The diagram below is a chromatogram of an extract from a supermarket curry sauce (S). Four reference samples of permitted colours have also been run on the chromatogram (E102, E110, E122 and E124).

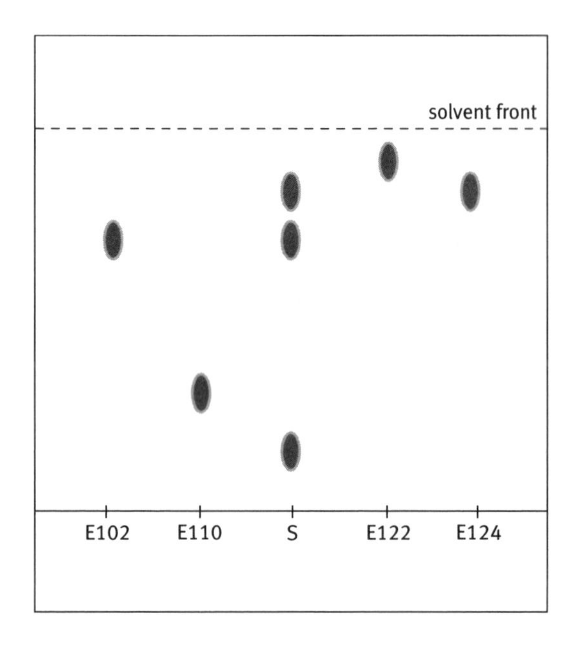

a How many coloured chemicals were there in sample S? ....

b Which permitted additives were present in the curry sauce? ....

c Calculate the R_f value for the spot that does not match any of the reference colours.

$$R_f = \frac{\text{distance moved by spot}}{\text{distance moved by solvent front}}$$

....

....

d Under the same conditions, the $R_f = 0.15$ for a banned colouring, Sudan 1. What does the chromatogram show about the colourings in the curry sauce?

....

....

e Suggest two ways which could be used to detect colourless additives on the chromatogram.

- ....
- ....

28 Gas chromatography

a Use the words in the box to label the diagram below, which describes gas chromatography (GC).

chromatogram	column packed with stationary phase	cylinder of carrier gas	detector
flow meter	mobile phase	oven	recorder
sample injected here	vent		

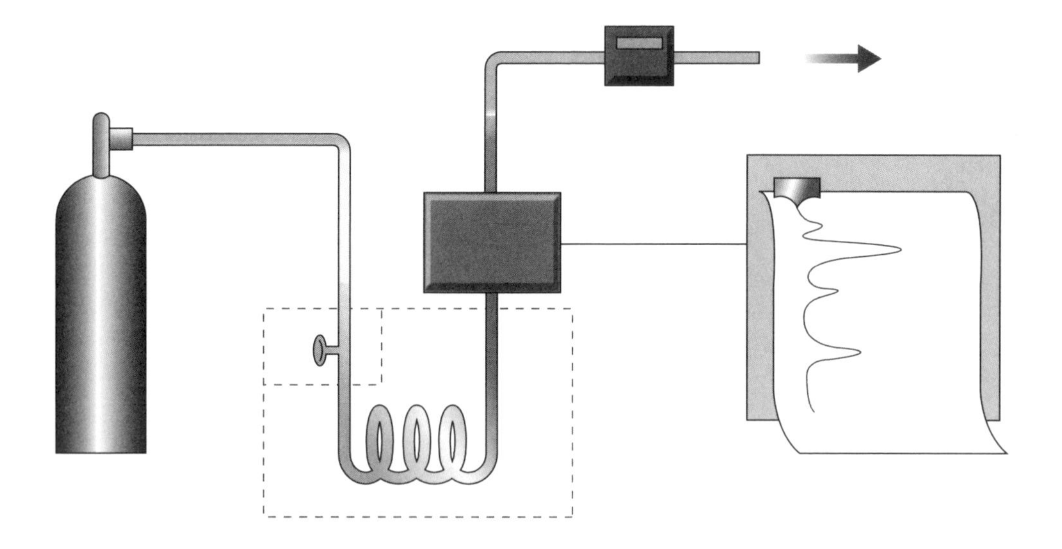

b The diagram below shows a gas chromatogram.

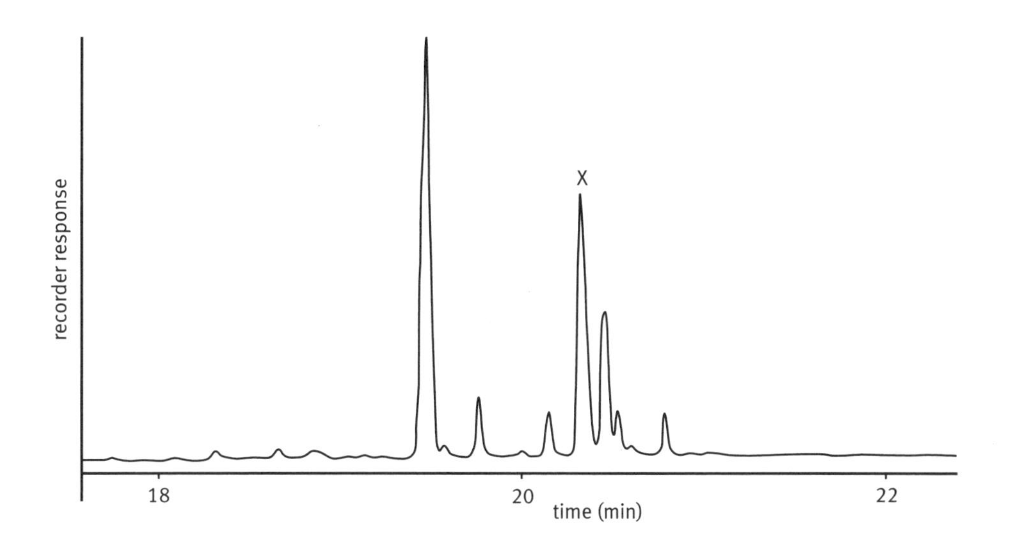

How many chemicals were there in the mixture injected into the GC instrument? ....

Which chemical was present in the largest amounts in the sample? ....

Estimate the retention time of chemical X. ....

....

29 Concentrations of solutions

a Label this sequence of diagrams to show how you would prepare a solution of sodium carbonate, Na_2CO_3, with a concentration of 10.6 g/dm^3, assuming that the volume of the graduated flask is 250 cm^3.

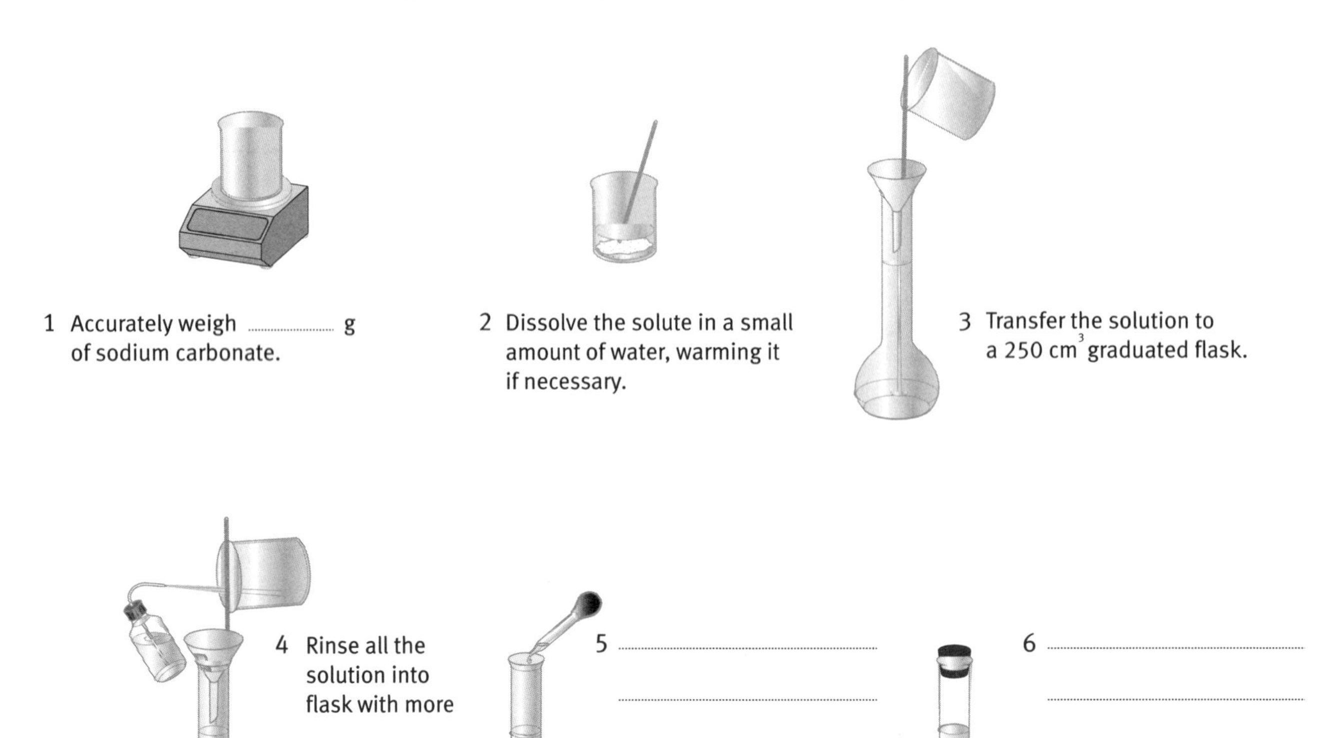

b Complete the table to show the concentrations of these solutions in g/dm^3.

Solution	Concentration in g/dm^3
20.0 g magnesium sulfate in 500 cm^3 solution	
4.5 g potassium hydroxide in 250 cm^3 solution	
0.5 g sodium sulfate in 10 cm^3 solution	
1.25 g silver nitrate in 50 cm^3 solution	

c Complete the table to show the mass of solute in these volumes of solutions.

Sample of solution	Mass of dissolved solute in g
100 cm^3 of a 25.0 g/dm^3 zinc sulfate solution	
50 cm^3 of a 10.0 g/dm^3 lead nitrate solution	
10 cm^3 of a 22.5 g/dm^3 magnesium chloride solution	
2.5 cm^3 of a 16.0 g/dm^3 barium nitrate solution	

30 Use of a pipette

A pipette is only accurate if it is used correctly. Suggest reasons for the following questions. Each question is designed to remind analysts about correct checks and procedures.

a Have you rinsed the pipette with the solution you are going to measure out? ....

....

b Have you made sure that there are no air bubbles in the narrower parts of the pipette? ....

....

c Have you wiped the outside of the pipette to remove solution on the outside of the glass before running out the liquid? ....

....

d Have you lined up the meniscus with the graduation mark correctly? ....

....

---

31 Use of a burette

A burette is only accurate if it is used correctly. Suggest reasons for the following questions. Each question is designed to remind analysts about correct checks and procedures.

a Have you checked that the burette is clean before you start? ....

....

b Have you rinsed the burette with the solution you are going to measure before filling it? ....

....

c Have you read the burette correctly and taken both readings? ....

....

d Have you left a drop hanging from the tip of the burette after running the solution into the flask?

....

....

32 A titration to analyse vinegar

a The diagrams below show steps in a titration to measure the concentration of acetic acid (ethanoic acid) in vinegar. Use the words in the box to label the diagrams. You may use the words more than once.

conical flask	burette	indicator	pipette	sodium hydroxide	vinegar

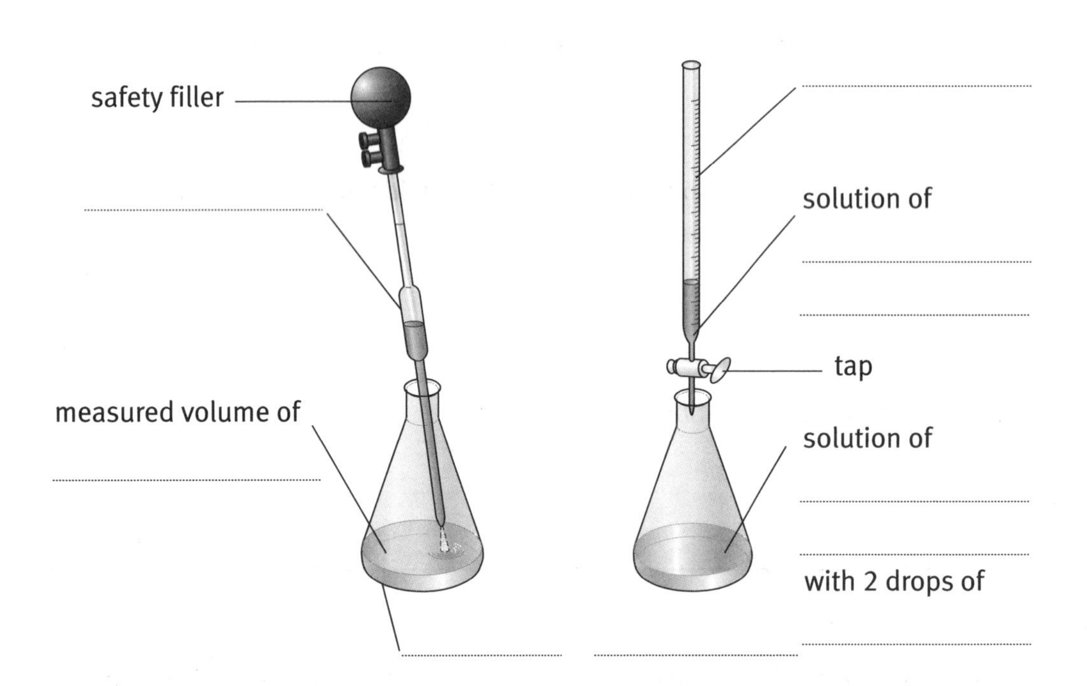

b The table below shows the results of a series of titrations to measure the concentration of acetic acid in vinegar. The flask contained 10.0 cm^3 vinegar and 3 drops of phenolphthalein indicator. The concentration of the sodium hydroxide solution in the burette was 20.0 g/dm^3.

	Rough titration	**Titration 1**	**Titration 2**	**Titration 3**
Second burette reading/cm^3 **First burette reading/cm^3**	17.5 0.0	22.00 5.00	19.00 2.10	20.10 3.20
Volume of NaOH(aq) added/cm^3				

i Complete the bottom row of the table.

ii Draw a ring round the values you use to work out an average value.

iii The average value for the volume of alkali added = ... cm^3

iv Use this formula to work out the concentration of the vinegar.

$$\text{Vinegar concentration } (g/dm^3) = \frac{3}{2} \times \text{NaOH concentration } (g/dm^3) \times \frac{\text{volume of NaOH } (cm^3)}{\text{volume of vinegar } (cm^3)}$$

Concentration of vinegar = ...

v The percentage of acetic acid by mass in the vinegar = ...

33 Interpreting titration results

An analyst carried out a titration to find the concentration of limewater. Limewater is a saturated solution of calcium hydroxide, $Ca(OH)_2$ in water. The analyst measured out 20.0 cm^3 samples of limewater and then carried out titrations with dilute hydrochloric acid. The concentration of the acid was 1.46 g/dm^3 HCl(aq). The average titre was 25.0 cm^3 of the dilute hydrochloric acid. Follow these steps to work out the concentration of calcium hydroxide in limewater.

a Write the balanced equation for the reaction which takes place during the titration.

....

b Work out the relative formula masses of calcium hydroxide and hydrochloric acid

(Relative atomic masses: Ca = 40, O = 16, H = 1, Cl = 35.5).

$Ca(OH)_2$ ....

HCl ....

c Calculate the mass of HCl in the 25.0 cm^3 of the dilute hydrochloric acid added from the burette.

....

....

d Use the equation and the reacting masses to calculate the mass of calcium hydroxide that reacts with the HCl added from the burette.

....

....

e This is the mass of calcium hydroxide in 20.0 cm^3 of limewater. Calculate the concentration of calcium hydroxide in limewater in g/dm^3.

....

....

34 Accurate quantitative analysis

Below are stages in a quantitative analysis. For each stage, show how this applies to a titration or explain why it is important.

- Measuring out accurately a specified mass or volume of the sample

- Working with replicate samples

- Dissolving samples quantitatively

- Measuring a property of the solution quantitatively

- Calculating a value from the measurements

- Estimating the degree of uncertainty in the results

35 Sources of raw materials

Inorganic compounds are obtained from never-lived sources. Organic compounds are obtained from living organisms and non-living sources. Sort the raw materials into the table.

air	bauxite	coal	crude oil	haematite	limestone	natural gas
phosphate rock	quartz	starch	rock salt	sugar cane	sunflower oil	
water	wood					

Never-lived sources	Once-lived sources	Living sources

36 Bulk and fine chemicals

a Fill in the missing names and formulae in the table of bulk chemicals.

Bulk chemicals	
Formula	**Name**
NH_3	ammonia
H_2SO_4	
	sodium hydroxide
H_3PO_4	phosphoric acid
C_2H_4	ethene

b Complete the table using these examples of fine chemicals.

carotene	citral	ibuprofen	glyphosate

Fine chemicals	
Type	**Example**
medical drugs	
agrochemicals	
food additives	
fragrances	

37 Regulation of the chemical industry

The UK government regulates chemical companies. For each of these areas, suggest a reason why it is important to have rules to protect the public, people at work, or the environment.

- Choice of raw materials for manufacturing ....

....

- Transporting chemicals ....

....

- Storing chemicals ....

....

- Getting rid of chemical waste ....

....

- Labelling of packs of chemicals ....

....

38 Chemical plants

Use the words in the box to complete the labelling of the diagram below, which summarizes key aspects of a typical chemical process in industry.

by-products	catalyst	energy	feedstocks	products	raw materials
reactor	recycling	separation	wastes	water	

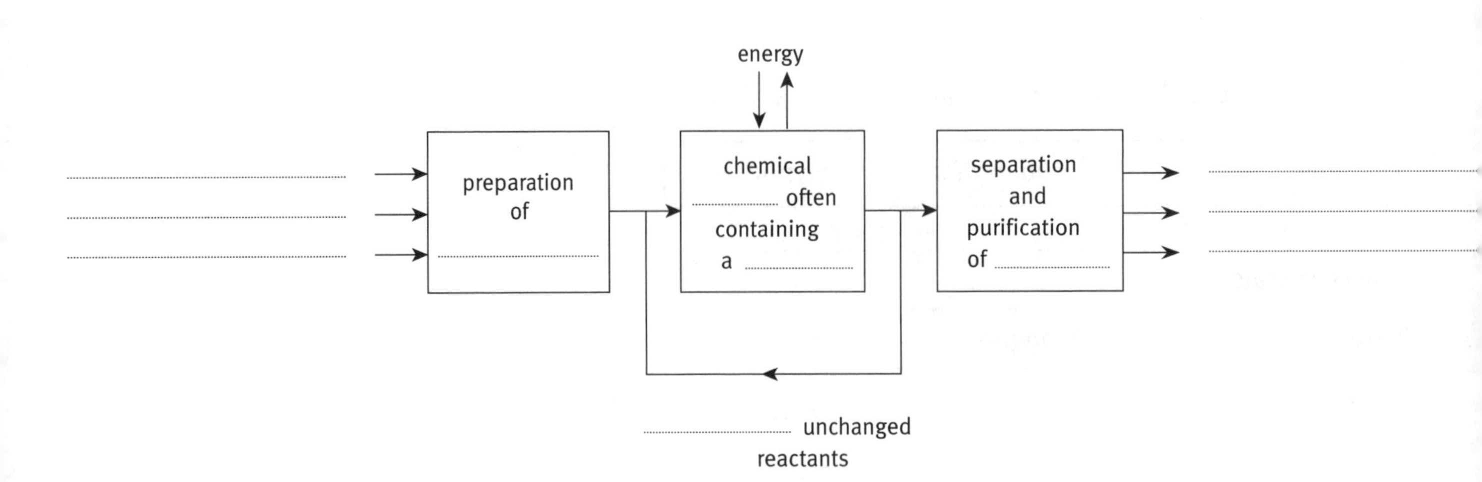

39 Types of feedstock

Use two colours for the key and then shade the areas in the grid with the colours to show which of these chemical feedstocks are renewable and which are not.

Key: ☐ Renewable ☐ Not renewable

ethene from refining crude oil fractions	methanol made from natural gas and steam	sulfur from the purification of natural gas
succinic acid from the fermentation of wastes from papermaking	sodium chloride (brine) from the dissolving of underground salt deposits	ethanol from the fermentation of sugars
oxygen from the air	lactic acid from the fermentation of beet sugar	naptha from distilling crude oil

40 Sustainable chemistry

Give examples from the chemical industry to show that the following can contribute to making chemical processes more sustainable.

- Avoiding chemicals that are hazardous to health ....

....

- Managing energy inputs and outputs ....

....

- Recycling chemicals ....

....

- Finding new uses for by-products ....

....

- Reducing waste products ....

....

41 Atom economy

There are two processes for making the chemical ethylene oxide. Complete the tables for the two processes and calculate the atom economies.

(Relative atomic masses: H = 1, C = 12, O = 16, Cl = 35.5, Ca = 40)

➲ Method 1: The two–step route

$$C_2H_4 + Cl_2 + H_2O \rightarrow CH_2ClCH_2OH + HCl$$

$$CH_2ClCH_2OH + HCl + Ca(OH)_2 \rightarrow CH_2\text{–}CH_2 \text{ (bridged by O)} + CaCl_2 + H_2O$$

Formulae of chemicals used	Symbols of atoms that end up in the product	Relative mass of atoms that end up in the product	Symbols of atoms that do not end up in the product	Relative mass of atoms that do not end up in the product
Totals				

Atom economy ....

➲ Method 2: One-step route with a catalyst

$$2C_2H_4 + O_2 \rightarrow 2CH_2\text{–}CH_2 \text{ (bridged by O)}$$

Formulae of chemicals used	Symbols of atoms that end up in the product	Relative mass of atoms that end up in the product	Symbols of atoms that do not end up in the product	Relative mass of atoms that do not end up in the product
Totals				

Atom economy ....

42 Catalysts

a Catalysts provide a different route for a reaction with a lower activation energy. Why does this make the reaction go faster?

b Industrial catalysts speed up reactions. Why does this mean that a more efficient catalyst can allow chemical plants to operate with smaller reactors?

c Good catalysts are highly selective. Why can this help to make a chemical process 'greener'?

d Give two examples of catalysts used in the chemical industry and state what they are used for.

- Example 1:
- Example 2:

43 Making ethanol from petrochemicals

Producing the feedstock, ethene

a Heating ethane at a high temperature breaks up the molecules and produces ethene, C_2H_4, and hydrogen. Write a balanced equation for the reaction.

....

The sources of ethane are natural gas and the distillation of crude oil.

Making ethanol from ethene

A mixture of ethene and steam under pressure combines to make ethanol in the presence of a phosphoric acid catalyst. About 5% of the mixture is converted to ethanol as the compressed gases pass through the catalyst.

b Complete the equation for the reaction

```
H         H                                      |    |
  \     /                                      — C — C —
   C = C      +  ..................  ——→           |    |
  /     \
H         H
```

c What is the theoretical atom economy for this reaction? ....

d Complete the labelling of this flow diagram for the process.

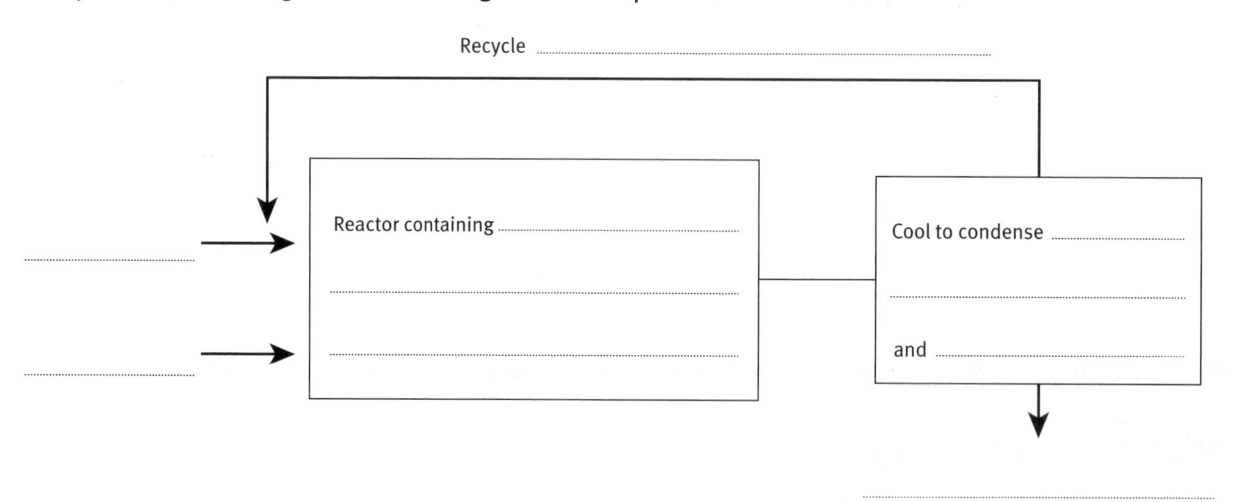

e Why is it necessary to recycle ethene in the process?

....

f Overall, the yield of ethanol from ethene is 95% of the theoretical yield. What mass of ethanol would be produced from 50 tonnes of ethene?

....

....

g Why does the ethanol produced need to be purified?

....

44 Making ethanol by fermentation of sugars

Feedstocks

a Give two examples of raw materials that might be used to make ethanol from biomass:

- a purpose-grown crop ....
- waste material ....

b Use the words in the box to complete the paragraph below.

biomass	catalyse	glucose	long chains	sugars

The chemicals in .... are polymers. They are .... of sugar molecules.

One example, cellulose, is a polymer of the sugar called .... ($C_6H_{12}O_6$). The industry uses water and acid to break down the polymers into simple sugars, such as glucose. After breaking down the polymers, the .... have to be separated from the acid used to .... the reaction.

Fermenting sugars with yeast

Fermentation converts sugars into ethanol and carbon dioxide. Enzymes in yeasts catalyse the reactions. Yeast is a living organism. Fermentation is an example of anaerobic respiration.

c Write a balanced equation for the fermentation of glucose.

....

d Fermentation with yeast works best at temperatures in the range 25 - 37°C. Suggest reasons why fermentation is slow:

- below this temperature range ....
- above this temperature range ....

e Why does fermentation slow down or stop if the alcohol concentration exceeds 14%?

....

f How is it possible to obtain ethanol solutions with a concentration above 14%?

....

45 Making ethanol from biomass with bacteria

Feedstocks

Breaking down biomass with acid can produce a wide range of sugars. These include six-carbon sugars such as glucose ($C_6H_{12}O_6$), and five-carbon sugars such as xylose ($C_5H_{10}O_5$). Yeast is good at converting six-carbon sugars to ethanol but not five-carbon sugars.

a Why is there a need to find new ways to convert sugars to alcohol?

- an economic reason ....

....

- an environmental reason ....

....

Fermenting sugars with GM bacteria

Scientists have used genetic modification to create a bacterium that can convert five-carbon sugars to ethanol. The diagram below shows a process which makes ethanol from biomass using this GM bacterium.

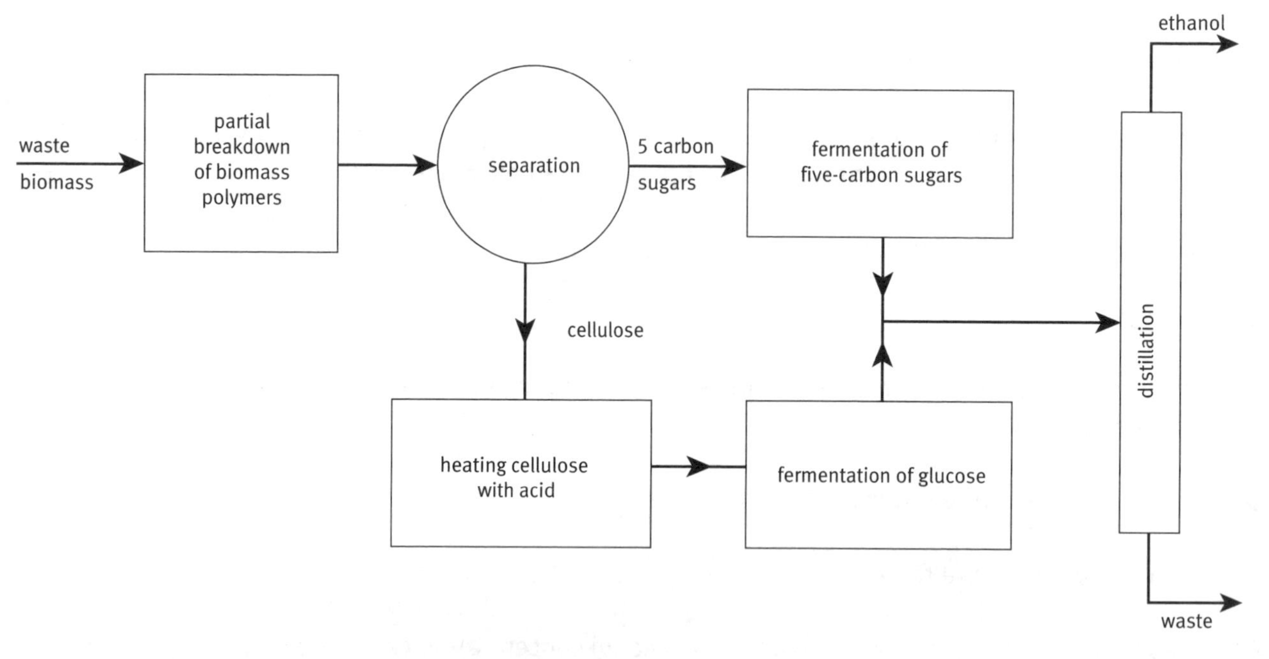

b What is the purpose of heating the cellulose with acid? ....

....

c Suggest a reason for fermenting glucose in a separate tank from xylose and other five-carbon sugars.

....

....

d What is the purpose of the distillation? ....

....

46 Uses of ethanol

Give examples to illustrate these uses of ethanol that is made on an industrial scale:

- as a fuel ....
- as a solvent ....
- as a feedstock for other processes ....

47 Ethanol manufacture and the environment

The diagram below compares, in outline, fuel ethanol from crops with fuel ethanol from oil. Crop-based ethanol could be carbon neutral.

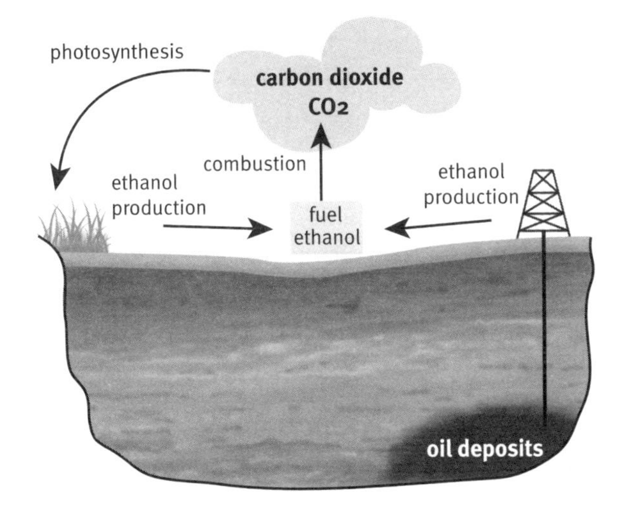

a Explain what the term 'carbon neutral' means.

....

....

b Why is fuel ethanol made from oil not carbon neutral? ....

....

c Why is it desirable to use fuels that are carbon neutral? ....

d Suggest two reasons why crop-based ethanol cannot be carbon neutral in practice.

- ....
- ....

e Identify two disadvantages of growing crops to make crop-based ethanol.

- ....
- ....

Observing the Universe

1 Observatories and telescopes

An observatory is a site used for observing objects in space. A telescope is any instrument that collects radiation from these objects for astronomers to study.

Complete the table, giving examples of telescopes and their locations.

Telescope	Type of electromagnetic radiation detected	Location
the Monument		
		Germany
	radio	
		low Earth orbit
Calar Alto		
	visible light	

2 How telescopes work

Telescopes can make things visible that cannot be seen with the naked eye.

Describe two different ways that they might do this. Use words from the box in your description.

distant source	telescope	weak radiation
detector	part of the electromagnetic spectrum	

3 Computer control in observatories

Tick the phrases below that complete this statement correctly. Tick more than one.

Computer control enables a telescope to

- track a distant source, collecting weak radiation from it, while the Earth rotates ☐
- scan a distant source, collecting data from each part of it ☐
- see clearly even when viewing conditions are poor ☐
- follow instructions from an astronomer who is not based at the observatory ☐
- move quickly and point precisely to another part of the sky ☐
- operate for more hours each year of its lifetime ☐

4 Converging lens

Complete the diagram to show what happens to the rays after passing through the lens.
Label the principal axis, focus, and focal length of the lens.

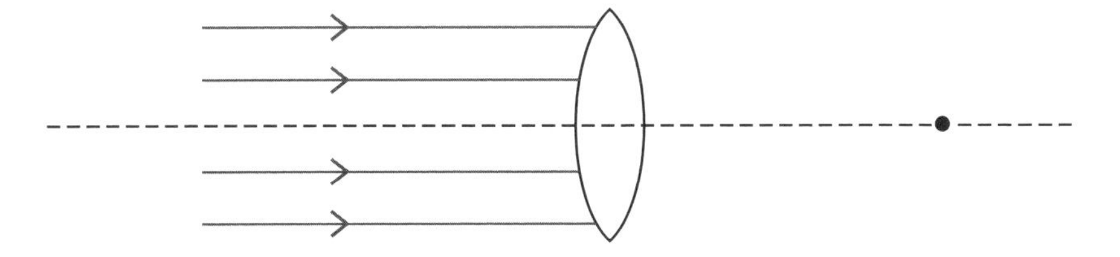

5 Converging lens shapes

Describe how the shape of a stronger lens differs from the shape of a weaker lens.

6 Power of a lens

a If you know the focal length of a lens, you can calculate its power. Give the equation for this.

b Calculate the power of a lens with each of these focal lengths:

i 0.5 m

ii 40 cm

iii 20 cm

iv 5.0 m

7 Describing images

Complete this statement using words from the box.

inverted	same size	real	bigger

What kind of image a converging lens makes depends on how far away an object is from the lens. An image can be described by its size compared with the object: smaller, the ....

as or ....

orientation compared with the object: upright or ....

image type: virtual or ....

8 Lenses in a telescope

a Label the eyepiece and objective lens in the diagram of a telescope below.

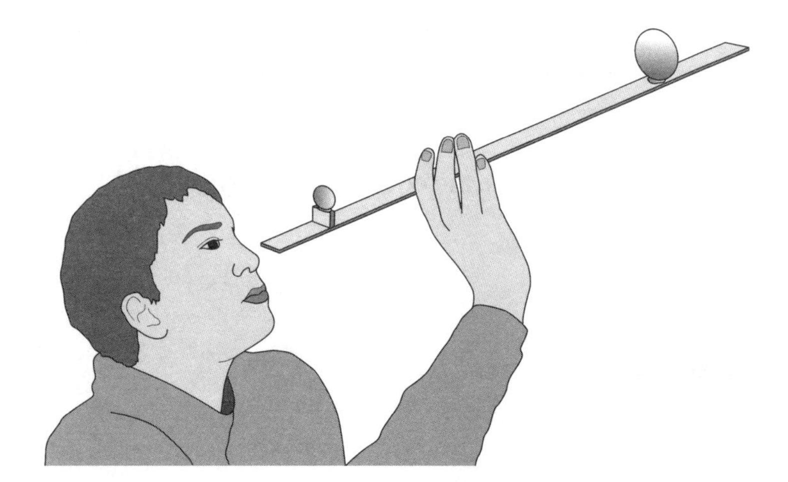

b Describe how the shapes of the two lenses compare.

....

....

9 Converging and diverging lenses

In these diagrams, label the converging lenses **C** and the diverging lenses **D**.

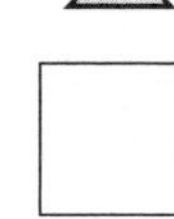
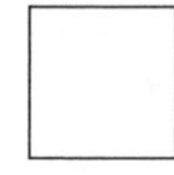

10 The magnification of a telescope

a Explain what is meant by the magnification of a telescope.

....

....

b Although no telescope can make stars look any larger, a telescope with greater magnification is still better for observing stars. Explain why.

....

....

c The magnification of a telescope can be calculated using this relationship:

$$\text{magnification} = \frac{\text{focal length of objective lens}}{\text{focal length of eyepiece lens}}$$

Complete the table below by calculating the magnification of a refracting telescope with each pair of lenses.

Telescope	Focal length of objective lens	Focal length of eyepiece lens	Magnification
A	50 cm	5 cm	
B	80 cm	5 cm	
C	5.0 m	5 cm	
D	1000 mm	4 mm	
E	2000 mm	10 mm	

d Which telescope provides the greatest magnification? ....

11 The aperture of a telescope

The aperture of a telescope is the light-gathering area of its objective lens. Give one reason why a telescope with a larger aperture is better than one with a smaller aperture.

....

....

12 Comparing lenses

The table below lists lenses, all made from the same type of glass, which may be used in making a telescope.

Lens	Focal length (mm)	Lens diameter (mm)
P	500	80
Q	250	120
R	25	60
S	50	100

a Which lens is the most powerful? ....

b Which lens would be thinnest (have surfaces with the least curve)? ....

c Which lens, if used as the objective lens, would give the brightest image? ....

d Calculate the magnification of a telescope made using lenses P and R.

....

....

13 Reflecting telescopes

Referring to the diagram below, explain a major problem with refracting telescopes. Explain also how this problem is overcome by using a mirror as the telescope objective.

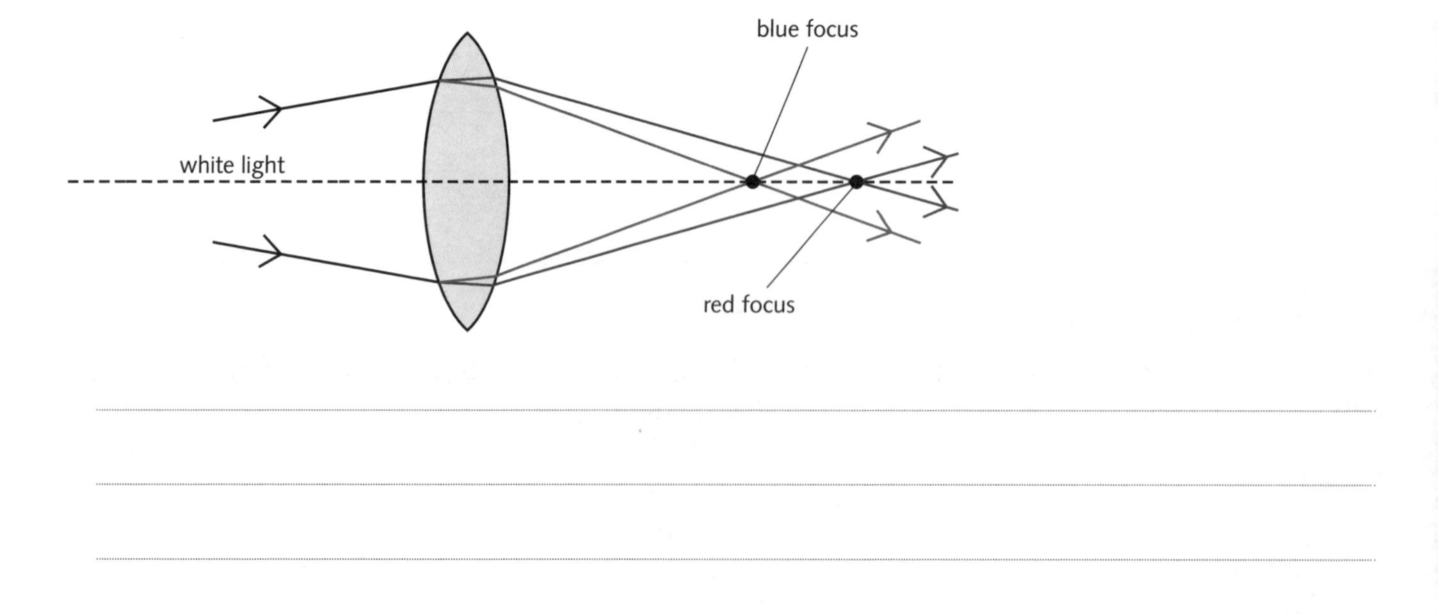

....

....

....

....

14 Mirrors for telescopes

Give three more reasons why most telescopes used by professional astronomers have mirrors as their objectives, and not converging lenses.

1 ....

....

2 ....

....

3 ....

....

15 Parabolic reflectors

A parabolic mirror is the most common shape for the objective of a reflecting telescope.

Complete the diagram to show what happens to the rays after striking the mirror. Label the principal axis, focus, and focal length of the mirror.

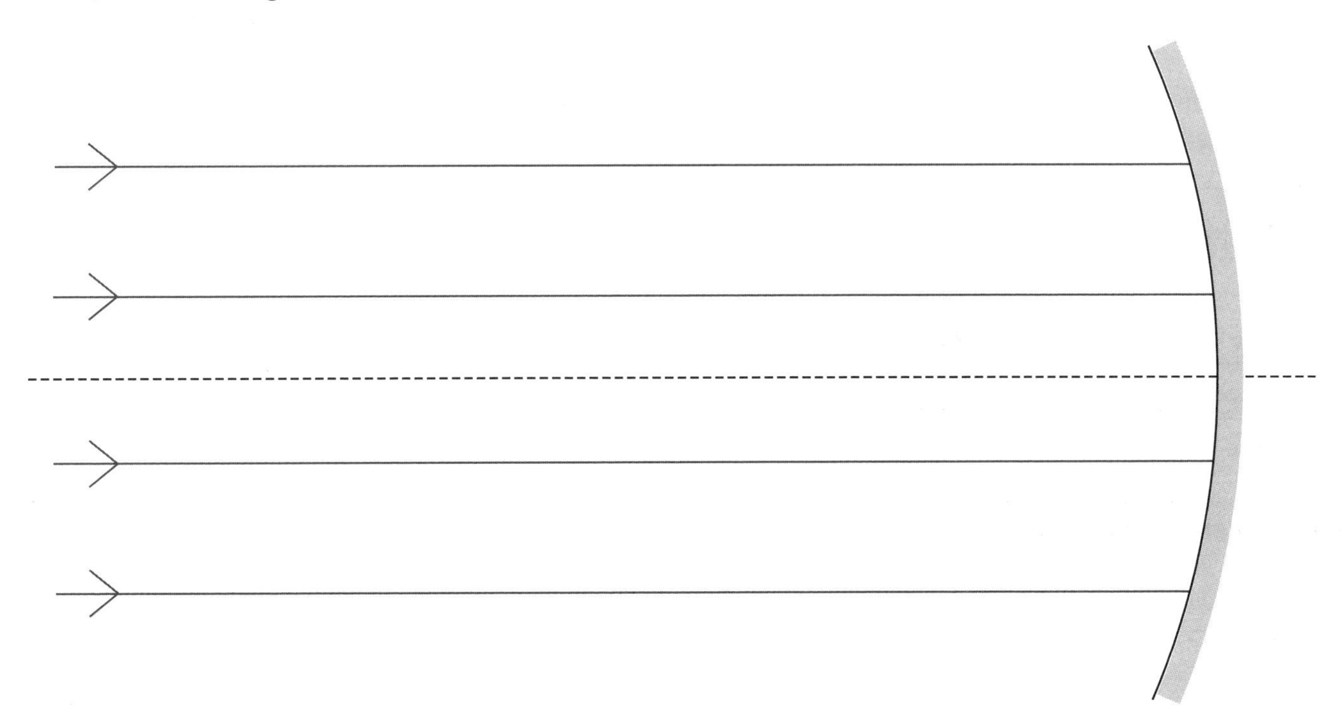

16 Wavelength and diffraction

Complete the diagram below to show what happens to the waves at these apertures.

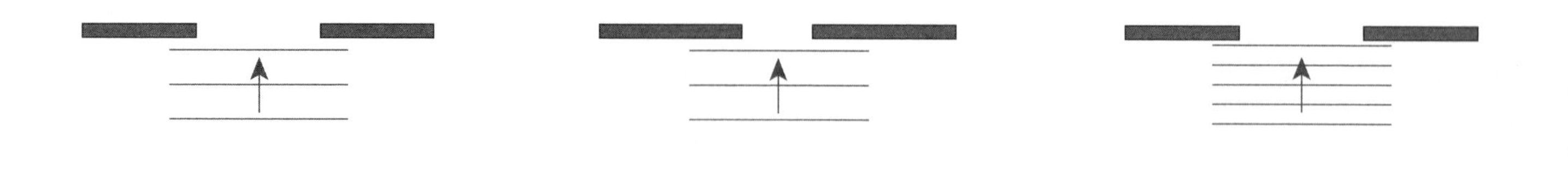

17 Wavelength and resolving power

Use words from the box to complete these sentences.

resolving power	diffraction	separate	electromagnetic	aperture	wavelength

The .... of a telescope is its ability to distinguish between two closely spaced objects so that they are recognizable as .... objects.

When the telescope .... is large in relation to the .... of the .... radiation being collected, astronomers will see more detail in an image. This is because of the effect of wave .... at any opening.

18 Images and resolving power

These diagrams show two light sources, observed through three different telescopes.

Draw lines to match each image to the telescope that made it.

High resolution telescope

Medium resolution telescope

Low resolution telescope

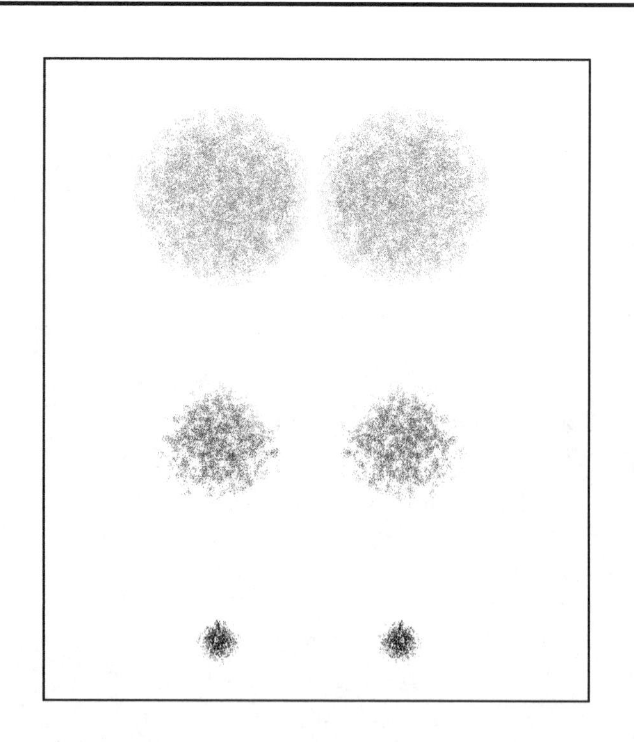

19 Large telescopes

Give two reasons why astronomers need to build very large telescopes.

1 ....

....

2 ....

....

20 Building telescopes

Describe two different engineering challenges in building large telescopes.

1 ....

....

2 ....

....

21 Parallel rays

Explain why light from any star arrives at a telescope as parallel rays. Use a diagram to help.

22 The image formed by a converging lens

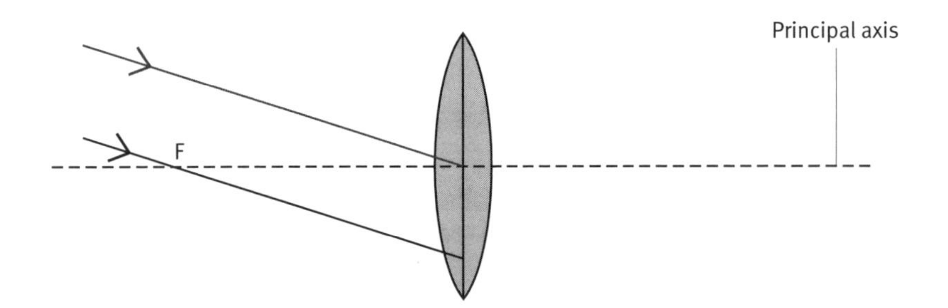

a The diagram above shows two rays from a distant star. One strikes the centre of the lens. The other passes through the lens focus before striking the lens. Show what happens to each ray, and add labels to describe the rule for each of them.

b Label the place where the lens produces an image of the star.

c Draw two more rays coming from the same star, and passing through the lens.

d Is the image virtual or real? Explain why.

....

....

23 An extended object

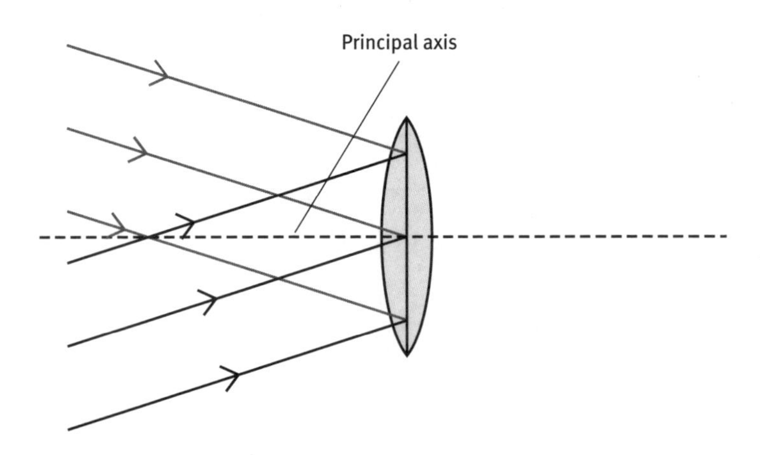

a The diagram above shows rays from a distant galaxy. The telescope objective lens gathers light from two sides of the galaxy. Assume the central rays both pass through the focus of the lens. Complete the rays to show where the lens produces an image of the galaxy.

b Annotate the diagram to explain the result.

c A galaxy is one example of an extended object that an astronomer might study. Give another example.

....

24 Refracting telescope objective

Explain why the objective of a refracting telescope should have a large diameter but be a weak lens.

---

25 The motion of stars

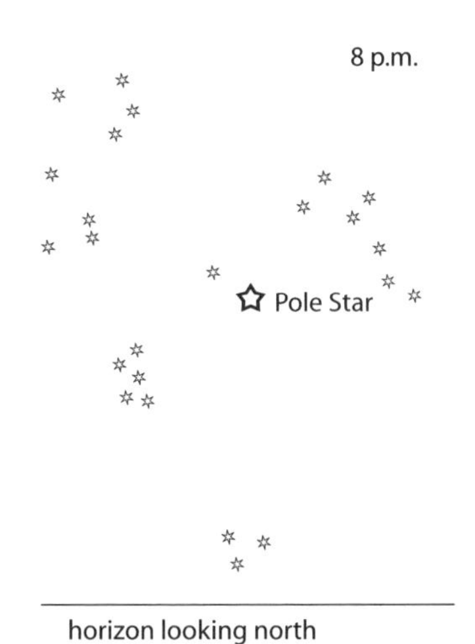

midnight

Pole Star

horizon looking north

a Describe how the stars appear to rotate during this 4 hour period.

b Explain why the stars appear to rotate.

c Why does the Pole Star not appear to move?

26 Sidereal and solar days

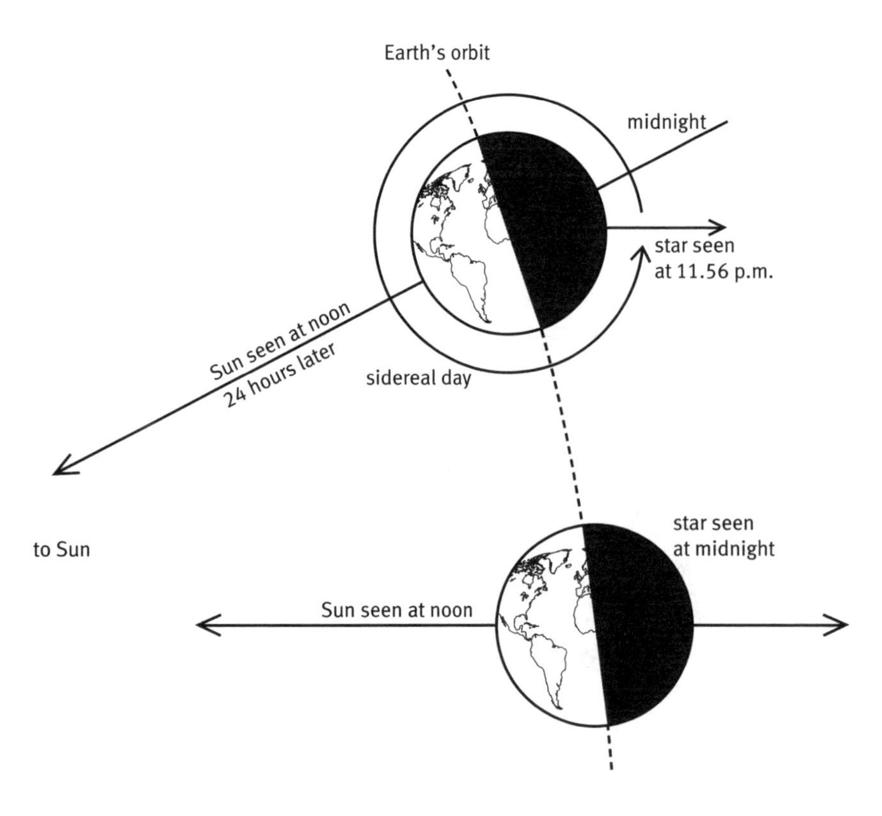

a Add labels to the diagram above, showing the time in hours and minutes
for a sidereal day
for a solar day

b Use the diagram to explain why any particular star rises 4 minutes earlier each day.

....

....

c Explain why a star will appear at exactly the same time and position in the night sky once every year. (Show that 4 minutes later every day, for 365 days, is about 24 hours – one full rotation of the Earth.)

....

....

....

27 Sun and Moon

Both the Sun and the Moon rise in the east, and cross the sky before setting in the west.

This sequence of diagrams shows the Moon moving east to west across the sky, but slipping back though the pattern of stars.

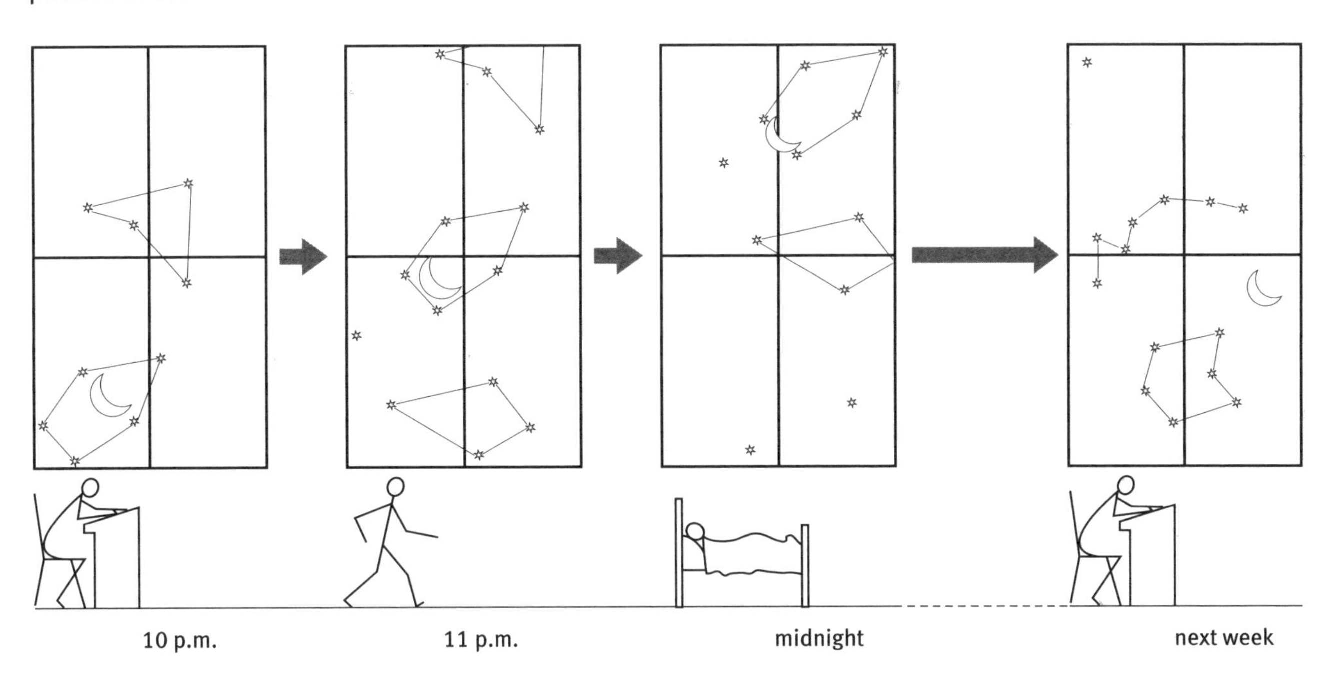

a Fill in the gaps, giving the times:

The stars appear to travel east to west across the sky once every ....

The Moon appears to travel east to west across the sky once every ....

b Explain why this happens, mentioning the Earth's rotation and the Moon's orbit of the Earth.

....

....

....

....

....

....

28 Phases of the Moon

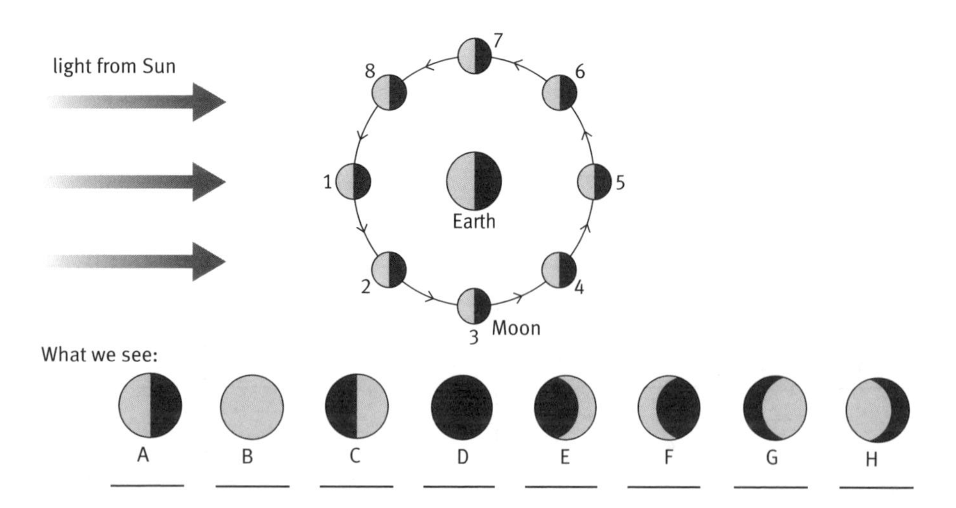

a Match diagrams A–H showing what we see with positions of the Moon 1–8 as it orbits the Earth.

b Write a short paragraph explaining why the appearance of the Moon changes in a regular way, in terms of the relative positions of the Sun, Moon, and Earth.

---

29 The position of a star

Draw a diagram and explain how you could use two angles to describe the precise position of an astronomical object.

30 Constellations and seasons

Different star constellations are visible in the night sky at different times of the year.

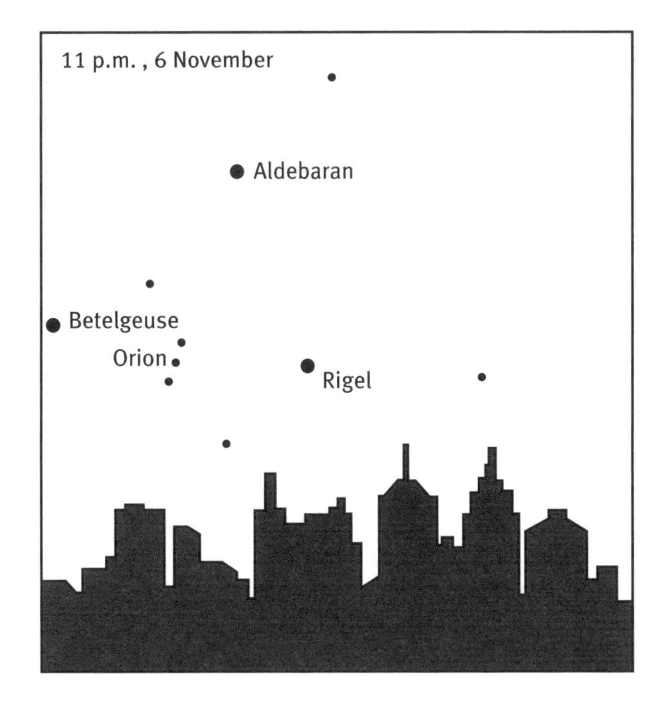

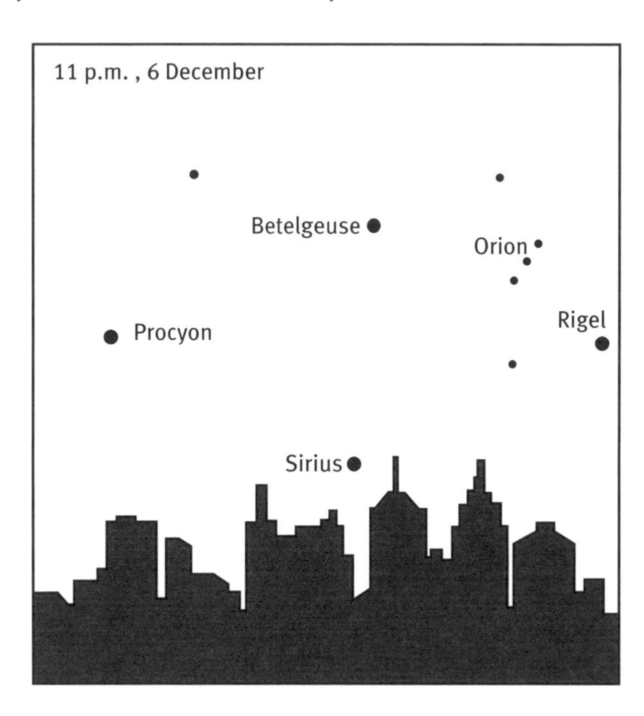

Explain this observation by annotating the diagram below, which shows the Earth orbiting the Sun and also shows the constellations of the zodiac.

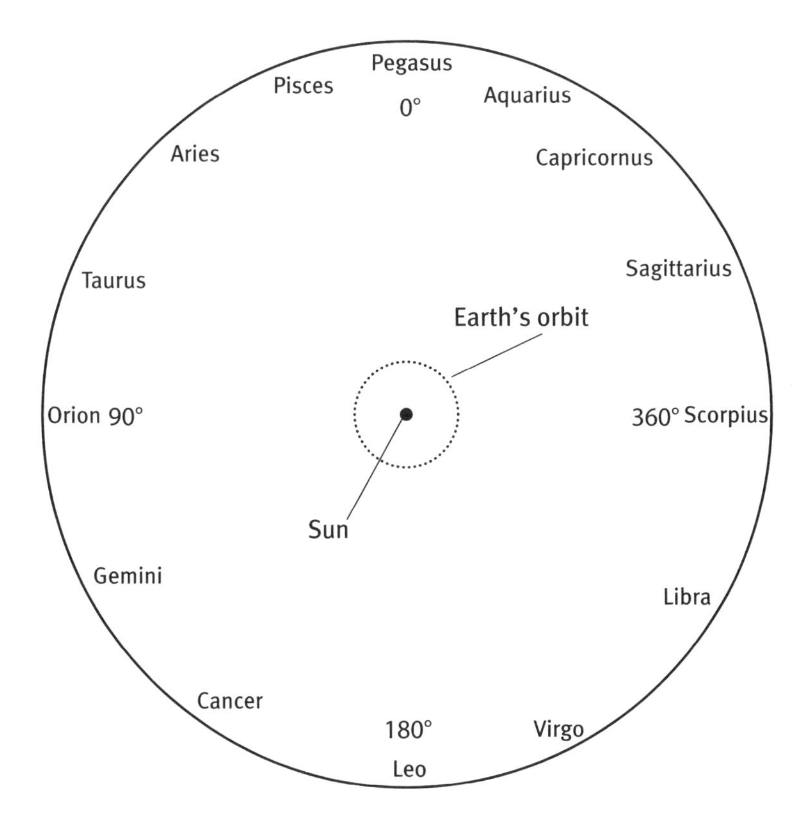

The zodiac is the set of constellations located around the ecliptic, i.e. around the extended plane of Earth's orbit of the Sun.

31 Retrograde motion of planets

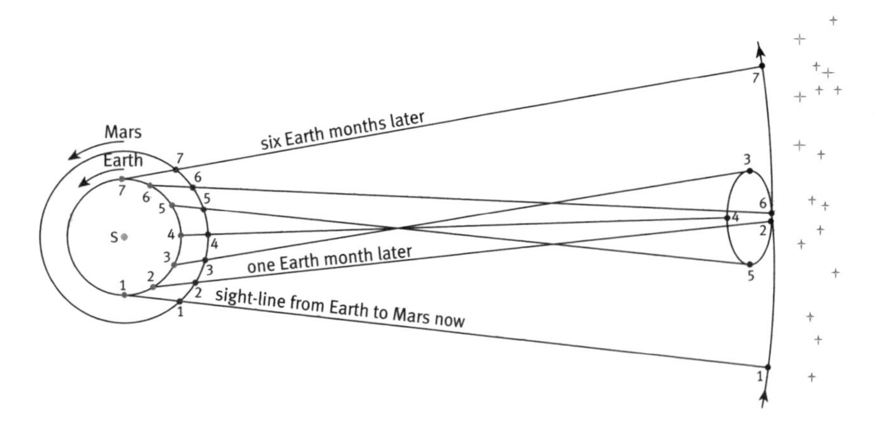

From months 1 to 3, Mars appears to move forwards. Then, for two months, it goes into reverse before moving forwards again. This is known as retrograde motion.

Write a short paragraph to accompany the diagram, explaining why Mars appears to move backwards (west to east) in the night sky for two months.

---

32 Eclipses

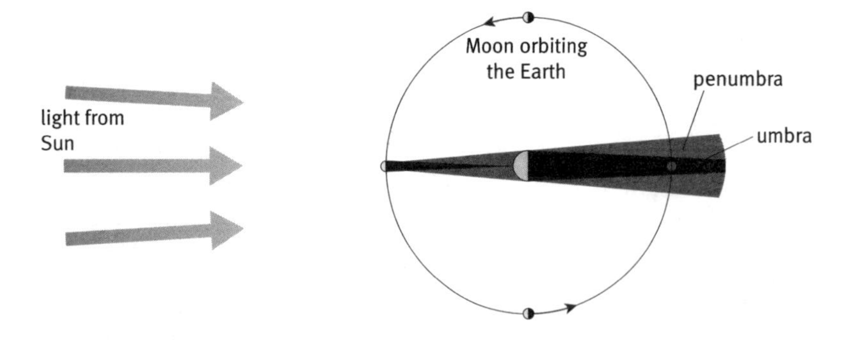

a Add labels to show the Moon's position when it
   i causes a solar eclipse
   ii causes a lunar eclipse

b Use the diagram to explain why lunar eclipses can be seen by many more people than solar eclipses.

33 Why eclipses are rare

Draw a diagram and annotate it to explain why eclipses are not seen every month.

34 Parallax

Using an everyday example, explain why nearby stars appear to move during the year against the background of distant stars.

35 Parallax angle

a Draw a diagram in the space below to define parallax angle.

b Use your diagram to explain why a star with a smaller parallax angle is further away.

36 Star distances

Complete the following sentences.

There are .... ° (degrees) in a full circle.

There are .... ' (minutes) of arc in 1o.

There are .... " (seconds) of arc in 1'.

A unit of distance based on the measurement of parallax is the ....

An astronomical object at a distance of 1 parsec has a parallax angle of .... This distance is equivalent to about .... light-year.

37 Parallax and parsecs

Complete the table by calculating each distance in parsecs.

Parallax angle (seconds of arc)	Distance (parsecs)
0.769	
0.1	
0.025	
0.0125	
0.06	
0.01	

38 Luminosity

The rate at which a star radiates energy is called its luminosity. Underline two factors that can affect a star's luminosity:

size twinkling parallax angle temperature

39 Observed brightness of a star

Explain why the observed brightness of a star (seen by an astronomer) will depend on both its distance and its luminosity. It may help to draw a diagram.

....

....

....

40 Comparing Betelguese and Orion

The constellation Orion contains the bright stars Betelgeuse and Rigel.

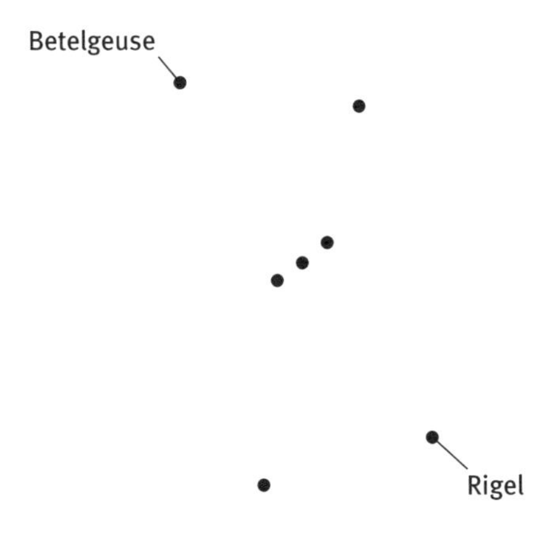

The following statements about these stars are all true.

Betelgeuse and Rigel are both about the same size.
Betelgeuse is red, while Rigel is blue-white.
Rigel gives out more than four times as much energy every second as Betelgeuse.
From Earth, Betelgeuse appears slightly brighter than Rigel.

Use this information to write a comparison of the nature of the two stars.

....

....

....

41 Star temperatures

Explain how astronomers analyse starlight to work out a star's temperature. Use the words in the box to help you.

electromagnetic radiation	frequencies	temperature	spectrometer
peak frequency	telescope	intensity of radiation at each frequency	

42 Star spectra and luminosity

The spectrum of a star can also be used to estimate its luminosity.

Tick the correct ending for the following statement.

Knowing the luminosity of a star and the intensity of its light at the telescope, an astronomer can calculate its

- temperature ☐
- distance ☐
- colour ☐
- galaxy ☐

43 The spectrum of a star

The graph shows the spectra produced by three different stars.

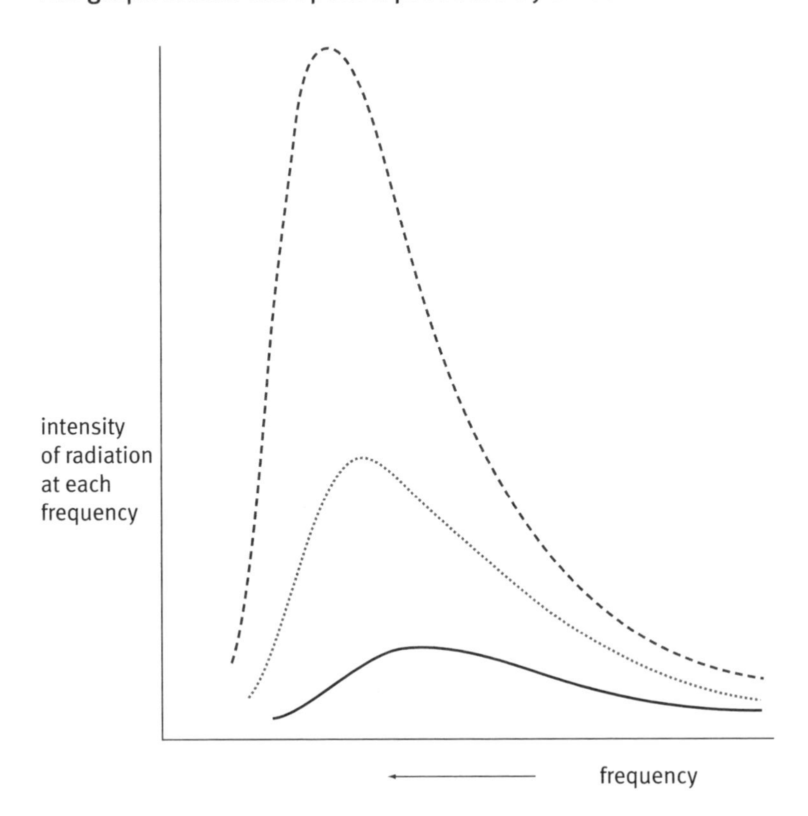

a Label the hottest star and the coolest star.

b What does the area under each graph indicate about the radiation from the star?

....

44 Cepheid variable stars

Cepheid variable stars were important in working out the distances to other galaxies.

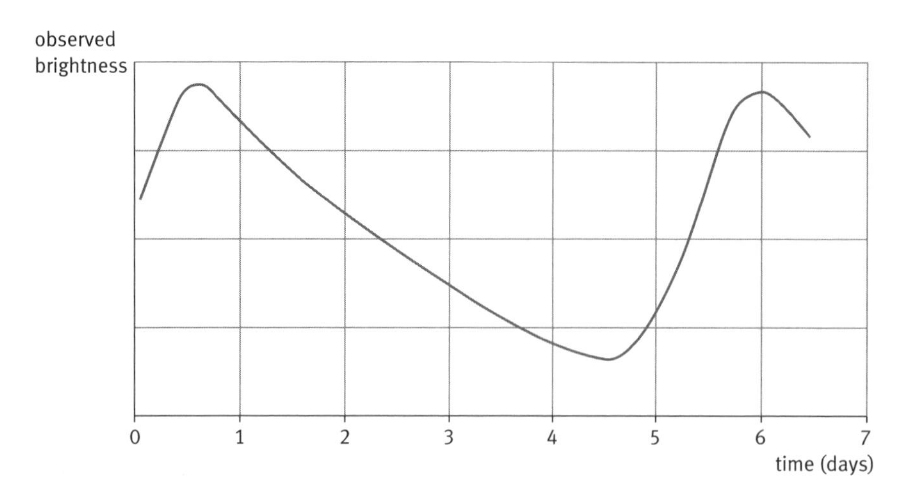

a The graph shows the brightness curve for a Cepheid variable star. Describe the pattern in its observed brightness.

b Henrietta Leavitt made a very important discovery about Cepheids. Draw a line linking the two variables which she found were related.

luminosity	observed brightness
temperature	period
distance	speed of recession

c The following sentences describe how astronomers use a Cepheid variable star to work out the distance to another galaxy. Number the boxes to put them in the correct order.

[ ] Use the period of variation of the Cepheid variable star to estimate its luminosity.

[ ] Produce a light curve for the Cepheid variable star and measure its period of variation.

[ ] Knowing both the luminosity of the star and the intensity of its light at the telescope, calculate the distance to the Cepheid variable star.

[ ] Look for a Cepheid variable star in the galaxy of interest.

[5] Take the distance of the Cepheid variable star as the distance to the galaxy.

In practice, astronomers would calculate the distance to many Cepheid variables stars in a galaxy to estimate its distance.

45 The scale of the Universe

a Use words from the box to complete the sentences.

nebulae	Curtis	Universe	Milky Way	galaxies	Shapley

In 1920 there was a famous debate between two American astronomers, Harlow Shapley and Heber Curtis, about the nature and size of the .... Central to the debate was the interpretation of thousands of fuzzy objects observed in the night sky, called .... The Milky Way includes nebulae and is much larger than previously thought, suggested .... Spiral nebulae are outside the ...., and are distant .... similar to our own, suggested ....

b How did Cepheid variable stars help to resolve this debate? Include the name of the astronomer responsible for this breakthrough.

....

....

....

---

46 Galaxies

The *Spitzer Space Telescope* is an orbiting infrared telescope. It was used to survey 30 million stars in the Milky Way, from which a group of astronomers was able to build up a picture of our galaxy published in 2005.

a What is a galaxy?

....

b Why was it essential to use an infrared telescope for this survey?

....

....

c Suggest why the survey was done by a *group* of astronomers.

....

....

d Complete the following sentences, using units in the box.

parsecs (pc)	kiloparsecs (kpc)	megaparsecs (Mpc)

Distances between stars in a galaxy are typically measured in ....

Distances between galaxies are typically measured in ....

47 Moving galaxies

Use words from the box to complete these sentences.

speed of recession	spectra	Hubble	away from	Cepheid variables

By analysing the .... of .... stars in 46 galaxies, ... discover that all other galaxies are moving .... ours. He also found that a galaxy's .... is proportional to its distance.

48 The Hubble equation

speed of recession = Hubble constant × distance

Complete the table showing data for different galaxies, using the Hubble equation.

Speed of recession	Hubble constant	Distance
5000 km/s	70 km/s per Mpc	.... Mpc
3500 km/s	.... km/s per Mpc	48 Mpc
.... km/s	2.3×10^{-18} s^{-1}	3.08×10^{21} km
2000 km/s	2.3×10^{-18} s^{-1}	.... km
3000 km/s	.... s^{-1}	1.23×10^{21} km

49 The composition of stars

The diagram shows the dark lines seen in the spectrum of visible light from a star.

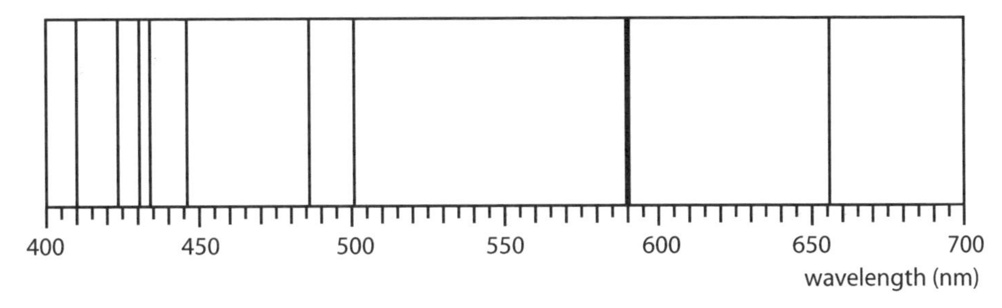

a Use the table below to identify the elements present in this star. Put a tick (✔) or a cross (✘) in every box in the last column.

Element	**Wavelengths (nm)**	**Present in the star?**
calcium	423, 431	
helium	447, 502, 588	
hydrogen	410, 434, 486, 656	
iron	431, 438, 467, 496, 527	
sodium	589, 590	

b A star is observed that contains only hydrogen and helium. Suggest and explain what this might imply about the star.

....

....

....

---

50 Energy levels and emission spectra

The diagram shows possible energy levels in an atom.

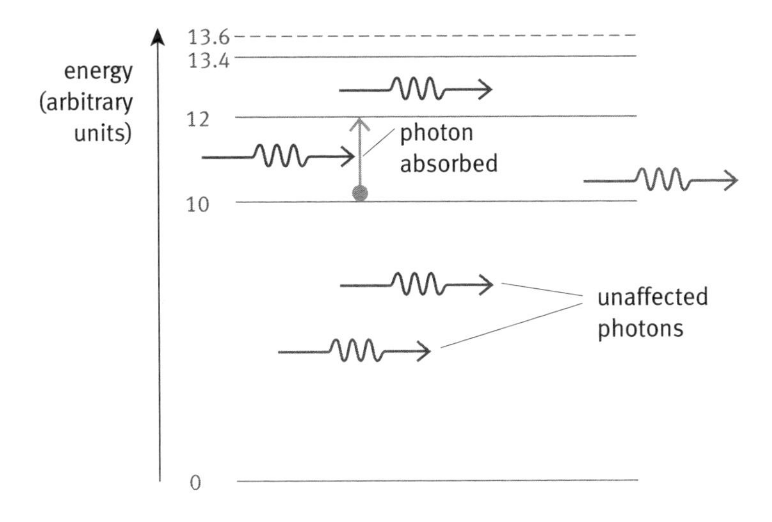

a Which subatomic particles are affected when atoms gain or lose energy by a discrete amount?

....

b Explain why this element emits light that makes a line spectrum rather than a continuous spectrum.

....

....

....

....

....

c The dotted line marked 13.6 represents the energy needed for ionization. An electron with this amount of energy, or more, would be able to escape from the atom. Use this mechanism to explain the difference between ionizing and non-ionizing radiations.

....

....

....

....

51 Atoms and nuclei

a The diagram below shows the apparatus used in Rutherford's alpha-scattering experiment.

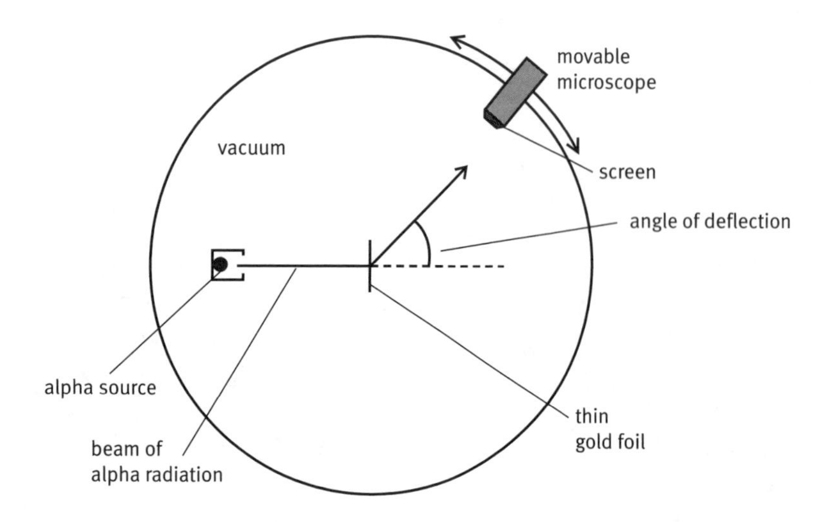

Why it is essential that the experiment is carried out in a vacuum chamber?

....

b Alpha radiation is directed at a sheet of gold foil. Describe the observations and conclusions from this experiment. (You may want to include a further diagram with the conclusions.)

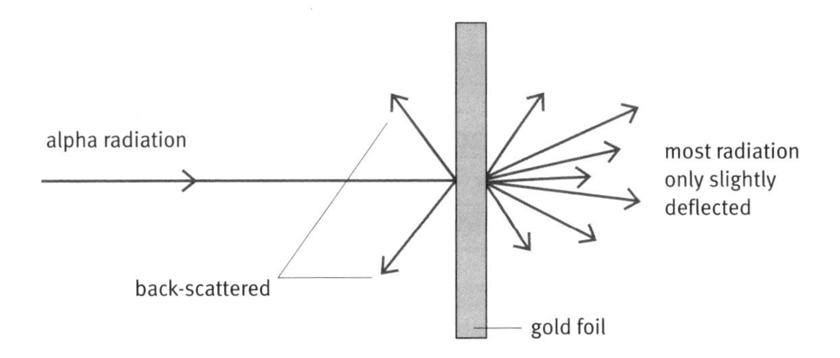

Observations:

....

....

....

....

....

Conclusions:

....

....

....

....

....

c Write these particles in the boxes below in order, from largest mass to smallest:

gold atom, alpha particle, gold nucleus, electron

largest

0.3 nm

smallest

52 The nucleus

a What two particles are found in the nuclei of atoms?

....

b Particles found in the nuclei of atoms are called nucleons. How does the mass of a nucleon compare with the mass of an electron?

....

c In a stable nucleus, two forces are balanced: the force that holds nuclear particles together and the force that tries to push some of them apart. Describe the two forces by completing the table.

	Name of force	Particles that the force acts on	Range of the force
Force holding particles together in nucleus			
Force pushing particles apart in nucleus			

---

53 Nuclear fusion

This explanation solved the mystery of the source of the Sun's energy:

> For nuclear fusion to occur, two nuclei must overcome their **repulsion** and get close enough for the **attractive force** to make them join together and make a new nucleus with a larger mass. The nuclei have **kinetic energy** before and after a fusion reaction. The process of nuclear fusion releases energy, so the total kinetic energy after a reaction is greater. Fusion takes place in the core of a star because of **conditions** found there.

Explain each of the terms in bold.

repulsion: ....

....

attractive force: ....

....

kinetic energy: ....

conditions: ....

....

....

54 The behaviour of gases

a What four quantities are needed to fully describe the properties of a sample of a gas?

....

b The kinetic model of matter says that all matter consists of tiny particles (often molecules) in motion. The following statements explain how a gas exerts pressure on the walls of its container. Draw lines to match the two parts of each statement.

The billions of molecules in a gas . . .	. . . is related to the temperature of the gas.
The speed of the molecules . . .	. . . causes a tiny force.
As the molecules move around, they . . .	. . . move around freely in what is mostly empty space.
Each collision with the walls . . .	. . . together produce gas pressure on the walls.
The tiny forces from molecular collisions with the walls . . .	. . . collide with each other and with the walls of their container.

c Use the model of molecular collisions to explain

i why the pressure of a gas increases when the volume of a gas is reduced, with its temperature constant

....

....

ii why the pressure of a gas increases with temperature, when its volume stays constant

....

....

iii why the volume of a gas increases with temperature, when its pressure stays constant

....

....

iv what a temperature of 'absolute zero' means

....

....

55 Temperature scales

a Complete this sentence.

The absolute zero of temperature occurs at .... °C or .... K.

b Complete the table by converting each temperature from one scale to the other.

Temperature (K)	Temperature (°C)
	100
35	
	510
173	
	−15
77	

56 Stars change

Use words from the box to complete these sentences.

data	colour	H–R diagram	luminosity	white dwarf
red giants	models	main sequence	small part	

Astronomers observe stars of quite different .... and .... When stars are plotted on a .... (a chart of luminosity against temperature), they fall into three main groups: main sequence stars, ... stars, and .... or supergiants. Linking .... about star populations to .... of how stars work, astronomers conclude that stars change, and that:

An average star spends most of its lifetime as a .... star.

A star may spend a .... of its lifetime as a red giant or as a white dwarf.

57 Main sequence stars

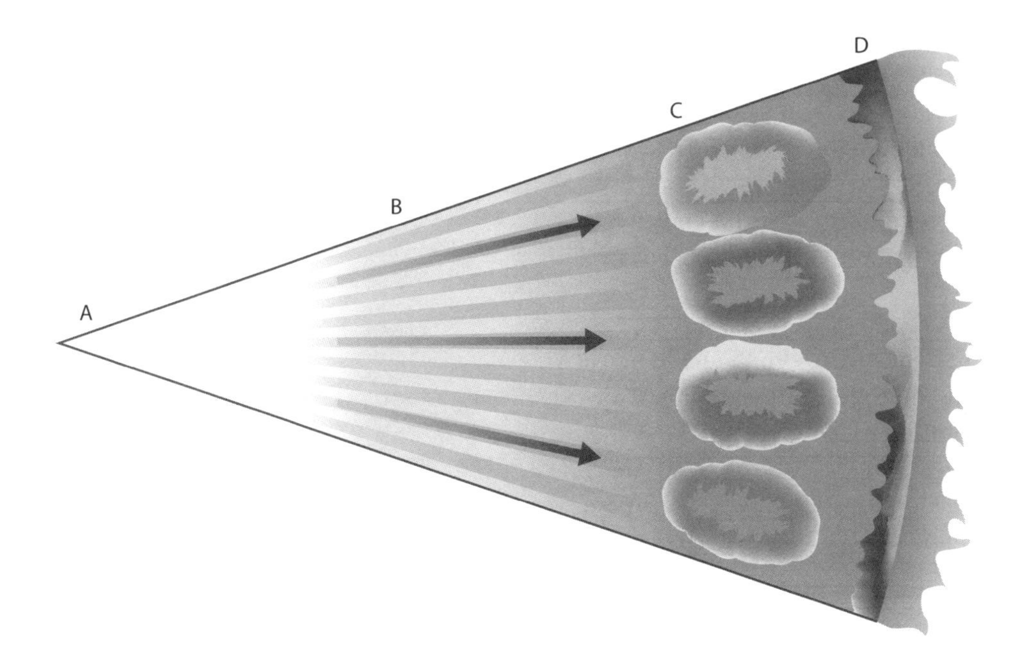

a The diagram shows the internal structure of a main sequence star.

Draw lines to match the labels and the descriptions of what happens in each part of the star.

Label	Part of the star	What happens there
A	photosphere	fusion of hydrogen takes place
B	radiative zone	energy is transferred by convection cells
C	core	energy radiates into space
D	convective zone	energy is carried by photons

b Fill in the blank to complete the sentence.

How long a star lasts in its main sequence phase depends on its .... and

....

58 Protostars

a Number the following statements in order, so that they describe the formation of a star with its solar system.

☐	Material further out in the disc clumps together to form planets.
☐	Eventually the temperature at the centre is hot enough for fusion reactions to occur and a star is born.
☐	A cloud of dust and hydrogen in space starts to contract, pulled together by gravity. It becomes a rotating disc.
☐	The temperature increases when the raw material is compressed, getting hotter and hotter at the centre.

b Use the kinetic model of matter to explain why the temperature in the centre of a protostar rises. Include in your explanation the role played by gravity.

....

....

....

....

c Explain why gravity gives any large mass of material a spherical shape.

....

....

....

59 Dying stars

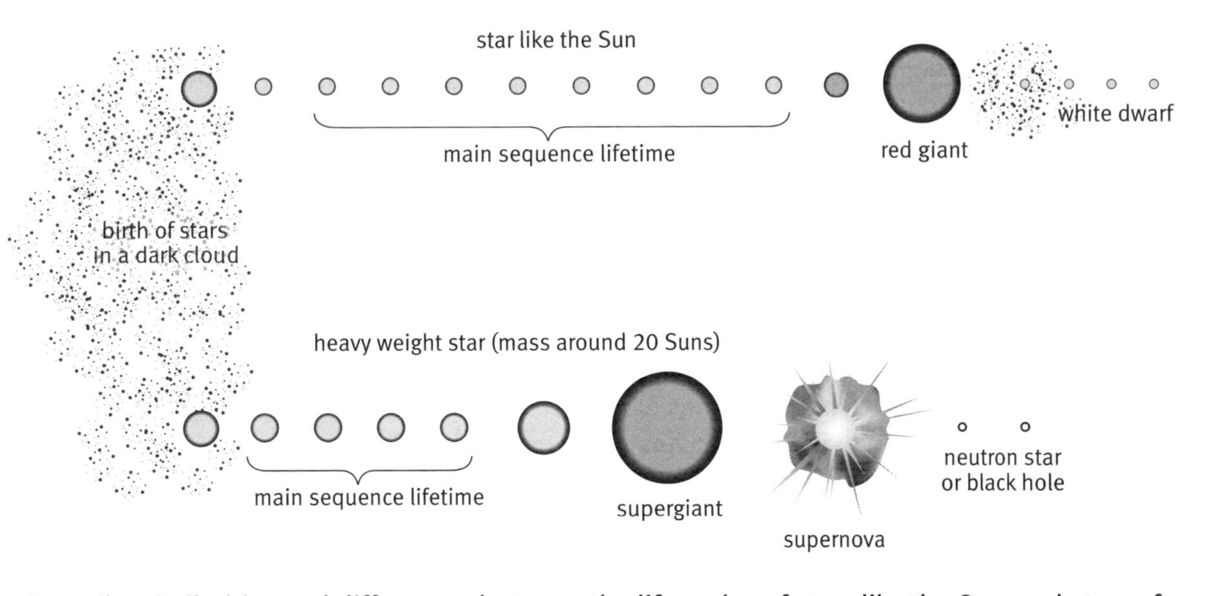

a Describe similarities and differences between the life cycles of stars like the Sun, and stars of much greater mass.

Similarities in their life cycles: ....

....

....

Differences in their life cycles: ....

....

....

b Use words from the box to complete these sentences.

kinetic	helium	decreases	gravitational	oxygen
red giant	hydrogen	carbon	increases	

As the .... of a main sequence star runs out, its core cools down and so its volume .... The collapse transfers .... energy to .... energy of helium nuclei, which means the star's core temperature .... This restarts the fusion process, with .... changing to nuclei of even bigger mass such as ...., nitrogen, and .... The energy this releases produces a .... or supergiant.

60 The final stages

a Fill in the blank to complete these sentences.

When a red giant runs out of helium, its mass is too small for gravity to compress its core and produce higher temperatures, and so fusion stops. The star shrinks into a hot ....

.............................., which gradually cools.

b The following statements describe what happens to supergiants. Number the statements in the correct order.

	The supernova remnant becomes either a neutron star or a black hole. Remnants with the biggest masses become black holes.
	When eventually the star produces iron, it runs out of nuclear fuel. The rate of fusion in the core decreases and pressure falls.
	The weight of outer layers of the star is no longer balanced by the core's pressure. The star dramatically collapses and then explodes as a supernova.
	Fusion in a supergiant continues to produce heavier and heavier elements, because gravity causes such high pressures in the core of massive stars.

---

61 Astronomy today

a Describe two ways that astronomers work with local or remote telescopes.

1 ....

....

....

2 ....

....

....

b What advantages does computer control of telescopes offer?

c Read the following statements about using telescopes outside the Earth's atmosphere. Put an A next to those that are advantages, and a D next to those that are disadvantages.

Advantage or disadvantage?	Statement
	They avoid absorption and refraction effects of the atmosphere.
	They are expensive to build and launch.
	They can detect radiation from astronomical objects in parts of the electromagnetic spectrum that are strongly absorbed by the atmosphere.
	Servicing relies on space programmes that astronomers cannot control.
	Orbit allows imaging from all parts of the sky.
	If things go wrong it is much harder to repair them.
	Instruments can quickly become out of date and are not easily replaced.
	Launching limits the size of the telescope.

d Give three reasons why international collaboration is common in astronomy.

1

2

3

62 Choosing a site

a Describe two factors that affect the quality of 'seeing' that influence the choice of site for astronomical observatories.

1 ....

....

2 ....

....

b List four factors of other types that are important in building and operating an observatory.

1 ....

2 ....

3 ....

4 ....